Unscientific America, 9/11, Sam Harris and Noam Chomsky

By Dr. Anab Whitehouse

Table of Contents

4

Unscientific America

Approximately, eight years ago, Chris Mooney and Sheril Kirshenbaum wrote: *Unscientific America: How Scientific Illiteracy Threatens Our Future.* Mr. Mooney is a best-selling author of non-fictional works exploring different aspects of science, while Ms. Kirshenbaum – after earning several masters degrees in marine biology and marine policy from the University of Maine (which is not too far away from where I currently live) – serves as the director for the non-partisan, nonprofit organization known as *Science Debate* which seeks to "restore science to its rightful place in politics".

Library Journal considered *Unscientific America* to be among the best Science-Tech books to appear in 2009. Moreover, the science advisor for President Obama – namely, John Holdren – highly recommended the foregoing book.

I purchased the foregoing title not too long after it came out when I was a member of a book club that featured material exploring different facets of science. However, as is often the case with me, a fair amount of time passed before I actually got around to reading that work.

During a section entitled: *From a Scientist and a Writer* – which amounts to a foreword for their publication – Mooney and Kirshenbaum describe an initiative known as ScienceDebate 2008 in which a physicist, philosopher, screen writer, and lawyer were brought together for the purpose of trying to induce members of the scientific community to contact politicians who were running for office and seek to persuade the latter individuals to begin taking seriously – by addressing – an array of policy issues involving science.

The two authors indicate that the aforementioned project exceeded everyone's expectations. More specifically, within a few months of organizing that event, more than 38,000 people were supporting their efforts, including many Nobel laureates, as well as scores of university presidents, numerous well-known scientists, and a variety of scientific organizations.

Nonetheless, despite the number of successful outcomes that ensued from the ScienceDebate 2008 initiative, the central thrust of that program appeared to be largely thwarted. More specifically, notwithstanding the fact that many scientists, educators, and scientific institutions had been sufficiently influenced by the foregoing project to begin actively reaching out to various politicians, unfortunately, candidates from both political parties – as well as the media – largely ignored the overtures of individuals from the scientific community and, as a result, failed to feature – or even include – various issues of science policy in their political campaigns.

Mooney and Kirshenbaum refer to scientists as a "reality-based community". For reasons that will be explored later in this chapter, such a moniker might be somewhat presumptuous ... at least in some cases.

In the meantime, one might keep in mind that not all science necessarily reflects reality (and as my book: *Evolution Unredacted,* documents, the theory of evolution tends to lend support to the foregoing claim). Moreover, there are many scientists who appear to be less interested – and, frequently, will admit as much – in discovering the nature of reality than they are in solving certain kinds of quantitative and physical problems and have found science to be a good means through which to bring their interests to operational fruition.

During the first part of Chapter One – entitled: 'Why Pluto Matters' -- the authors of *Unscientific America* comment on the existence of a dangerous fault line that they believe runs through much of American life in which competing theories of reality, like so many conceptual tectonic plates, push up against one another, creating complex dynamics that could release a great deal of destructive potential at any given time. The foregoing pressures stem from, on the one hand, the fact that for more than half a century, hundreds of billions of dollars have been spent on establishing and operationally funding an assortment of government-based and academic-oriented laboratories (and this doesn't take into account the trillions of dollars that have been spent or the research and development of military weapons that seek to exploit the findings of science), and, yet, on the other hand, Mooney and Kirshenbaum decry the fact that a disturbingly high number of Americans – at least from the perspective of the authors – continue to resist, if not reject, a variety of fundamental scientific principles ... such as "the scientifically undisputed explanation of the origin of our species and the diversity of life on Earth" (page 3) known as the theory of evolution.

As has been noted previously (both in this book and elsewhere in my writings), one could acknowledge that the theory of evolution is "the scientifically undisputed explanation" for the origins of all species, but this might be more of a reflection on the problematic state of science when it comes to the theory of evolution than it is an admission that what is considered to be a scientifically undisputed explanation necessarily gives expression to either truth or reality. Moreover, one might challenge the claim that the theory of evolution is the "scientifically undisputed explanation" for the origins of all species because there are scientists – such as Michael Behe, a biochemist at Lehigh University – who do dispute the scientific viability of the explanation to which the theory of evolution gives expression.

To be sure, for a variety of proffered reasons, scientists (e.g., Kenneth Miller – a cell biologist at Brown University) do criticize and reject the position of Professor Behe vis-à-vis the theory of evolution (whether, or not, those proffered reasons are actually viable is another matter). Nonetheless, the very fact that there are scientists – whether they are right or wrong in what they have to say – who do dispute that the theory of evolution is an adequate explanation for the origins of all species tends to belie the foregoing contention of Mooney and Kirshenbaum that the theory of evolution is a "scientifically undisputed explanation."

Of course, if one is so inclined, one can restrict use of terms such as: "Scientist," "science," and "scientific" to situations in which only those individuals and understandings with which one agrees will be considered to be deserving of such descriptions. However, doing so would tend to prejudicially distort the nature of science since many theoretical positions, ideas, and hypotheses often are advanced when various aspects of the material world are explored, yet determining where the truth lies in any given case is not always easy and clear-cut even if – often for either arbitrary reasons or for reasons that later turn out to be problematic – the consensus of scientific opinion might be, at least for a time, oriented around one conceptual position rather than another.

For example, many physicists, for relatively arbitrary reasons, accepted Bohr's Copenhagen interpretation of quantum mechanics. The reasons being alluded to in the previous statement are arbitrary because Bohr never actually proved that his understanding of things was correct. Instead, he was merely able to point out problems with a number of proposals that had been put forth at various Solvay gatherings by Einstein ... proposals that were expressed in the form of thought experiments that were intended to challenge the viability of the Copenhagen interpretation of quantum mechanics.

In addition to various comments concerning the sad status of the attitudes of large segments of the population in America toward the theory of evolution, the authors of *Unscientific America* also proceed to run through a litany of related problems that science and scientists face in America. For instance, they indicate that a study conducted by the *Project for Excellence in Journalism* discovered that during any given five hour period of cable news, one was not likely to encounter more than a minute, or so, of science coverage while being exposed to: 26 minutes of crime, 12 minutes of news items involving disasters and accidents of one kind or another, and 10 minutes worth of entertainment and celebrity news.

Research also has revealed that during the sixteen-year period between 1989 and 2005, the number of newspapers that contained a section on science were reduced from 95 to 34, a nearly two-thirds reduction in featured coverage. The *Boston Globe* joined the foregoing exodus in 2009 when they discontinued their highly respected section on science.

Furthermore, the National Science Foundation gathered data indicating that approximately only 15% of the American public is committed to pursuing various issues concerning science or news about science. Most of the rest of the American public seems to be steeped in one form, or another, of scientific illiteracy.

Thus, despite the fact that science and scientists possessed a great deal of cultural authority following World War II, nonetheless, for a variety of reasons, such prestige has steadily been eroded over the last 70 years. Some of the reasons underlying the loss of cultural authority that once had been enjoyed by scientists are a function of the previously noted changes in the nature of media coverage – or lack thereof.

The aforementioned decline in prestige among scientists also has to do with the way in which science is taught in grammar and high schools (especially when such "teaching" is conducted by individuals who lack true competency in science and, therefore, probably should not be conducting classes in science to begin with). Finally, still other reasons for the decline in prestige of the scientific community that was noted earlier have to do with the way in which many scientists have permitted themselves to become entangled in various kinds of conflicts of interest in which they have preferred their own financial and political interests to the possible best interests of the general public.

During his celebrated 1959 talk concerning two cultures – namely, science and humanism -- C.P. Snow explored several dimensions of the foregoing sort of disjointed and, frequently, contentious relationship. Among other things, he indicated that the foregoing two communities seemed to have little understanding of one another and, in addition, often were contemptuous toward whichever of the two cultures they did not consider to be their own.

The authors of *Unscientific America* believe that at least part of the solution for addressing the issue of scientific illiteracy among Americans rests with working to enhance the quality of the communication that takes place between the community of scientists and the rest of society. Among other things, the two authors felt that as a result of such factors as over-specialization within science, the processes, properties, principles, problems and potential of science were not being properly communicated to the rest of society, and, therefore, over time, science and scientists suffered a loss of relevance, significance, and influence in the minds of the American public.

However, there might be another reason why scientists have lost much of their cultural authority among Americans. More specifically, for a variety of reasons, many Americans no longer trust scientists to serve as objective, honest brokers of truth concerning the nature of reality.

To be an objective, honest broker of truth does not necessarily mean that one's understanding of some facet of reality is correct or true. Being an objective, honest broker of the truth requires that a person's efforts to acquire insight into the nature of some aspect of existence be rooted in a rigorous process that is transparent, open, not intended to evade difficult problems, or mislead and distort (through commission or omission) with respect to relevant issues, as well as be critically and fairly responsive to evidence.

Mooney and Kirshenbaum do indicate that they consider scientists such as Richard Dawkins and Sam Harris to be zealots who might be more interested in using science as a means for promoting their New Atheism than they are committed to uncovering the truth. Moreover, the authors of *Unscientific America* also indicate that such ideological extremists tend to undermine efforts to find common conceptual ground because the aforementioned sorts of individuals seem to be more interested in discovering reasons for continuing to be combative rather than engaging in discussions that are sincerely dedicated to seeking the nature of truth no matter where this might lead.

On the other hand, Mooney and Kirshenbaum claim there are many individuals who reject bedrock scientific discoveries such as the theory of evolution because the latter individuals "... wrongly consider such knowledge incompatible with faith." (Page 9) Unfortunately, the two authors of

Unscientific America never explain in just what way the kind of knowledge to which they are alluding is, supposedly, compatible with faith, nor do they explain how so many people seem to have arrived at such an incorrect understanding concerning the theory of evolution.

Whatever one might think about the truth of either some form of evolution or creationism, there appears to be a fundamental difference between, on the one hand, worldviews which maintain that everything (in physics, chemistry, and biology) is, at some point, a function of random events, and, on the other hand, conceptual frameworks which contend that events occur in accordance with determinate principles of Divine governance. To be sure, there are some scientists -- such as Kenneth Miller -- who believe in both God as well as the theory of evolution, and, in the process, seem to suppose that the universe – and, therefore, God -- operates in accordance with, among other things, the principle of quantum indeterminacy, and as a result, seek to portray God and random events as being mutually compatible with one another, but the foregoing efforts seem more like a process of trying to square the circle rather than constituting a viable scientific point of view.

Consequently, one wonders to what extent Mooney and Kirshenbaum can be trusted as honest brokers of the truth – that is, why should they be believed -- when they try to claim that those who believe in God are wrong when the latter individuals consider the theory of evolution – as currently understood with the science community -- to be incompatible with faith. In other words, the two authors of *Unscientific America* don't appear to be serving as honest brokers concerning the search for truth when considering the nature of the relationship between the theory of evolution and the existence of God because they seem to distort the actual nature of that relationship in order to present science – at least as it is understood and practiced by the vast majority of scientists -- in a less antagonistic, more moderate, and "reasonable" light.

Unfortunately, there is a much more problematic dimension associated with various facets of science and so-called scientists than whether, or not, science and faith can be reconciled. This problematic dimension has to do with the way in which all too many scientists go about pursuing science – or failing to do so – in contexts that entail threatening possibilities for their careers, reputations, financial interests, and/or physical safety.

The events of 9/11 constitute such a context. Those events give expression to a challenge for anyone – whether scientists or non-scientist – who wishes to claim that he, she, or they are interested in seeking the truth of things.

Throughout the book by Mooney and Kirshenbaum, issues such as the theory of evolution and global warming are mentioned again and again as being pertinent to the task and challenge of trying to rehabilitate the sense of significance, relevance and influence that is associated with science in the minds of the American public. Yet, a rigorous discussion concerning the scientific issues surrounding 9/11 is completely absent from the contents of the foregoing book, and one can't help but wonder if the "reasons" why that sort of discussion is absent from the pages of *Unscientific America* might play more of a role in inducing Americans to be scientifically illiterate than does anything that Mooney and Kirshenbaum might have to say concerning why they believe such illiteracy exists and how that problem could be resolved ... indeed, the absence of the 9/11 issue in *Unscientific America* would seem to be one more indicator that there are individuals within the scientific community who cannot necessarily be trusted to be honest brokers of the truth concerning certain facets of reality ... that is, the efforts of such people to acquire insight into the nature of some aspect of existence is not necessarily rooted in a rigorous process that is transparent, open, unintended to evade difficult problems, or mislead and distort (through commission or omission) with respect to relevant issues, as well as be critically and fairly responsive to evidence.

The process of becoming, or being, an honest broker in matters of truth is often filled with a variety of difficulties. For instance, individuals often have to struggle in order to overcome blind

16

spots in their understanding of things so that they might serve as an honest broker of events – scientific and otherwise.

However, some individuals seem unwilling, or incapable, of making the sorts of conceptual, methodological, epistemological and/or moral adjustments that are necessary to be able to engage issues in an objective, rigorous, and critically reflective manner. The discussion that begins on page 15 involves an inquiry into three individuals and their respective manners of engagement of issues involving 9/11.

One of the individuals being alluded to in the foregoing paragraph – namely, Peter Michael Ketchum -- was able to make the kinds of conceptual and emotional adjustments that enabled him to recover certain aspects of his ability to be able to try to serve as an honest broker of truth within the scientific community in matters involving 9/11. Unfortunately, the other two individuals that are discussed in the material that follows – namely Sam Harris and Noam Chomsky – do not appear to have been able to make the same kinds of adjustments as were navigated by Mr. Ketchum, and, as a result, they do not, yet, appear to have been able to rediscover and re-capture the qualities that are necessary to be able to serve as honest brokers of truth in the matter of 9/11 … and, perhaps, in relation to other issues as well.

Consequently, Sam Harris and Noam Chomsky seem to have become deeply entangled in the problems associated with the ramifications of what being truly "unscientific" in America entail. In other words, Dr. Harris and Professor Chomsky tend to behave like individuals who, in any given case – such as 9/11 -- are unwilling, or incapable of, objectively searching for evidence, judiciously analyzing the significance of that evidence, and accurately identifying whatever truth such evidence reveals.

[[**Note**: There is a relatively small amount of repetition that occurs during the ensuing discussion. This is due, in part, to the fact that Sam Harris and Noam Chomsky often make the same, or similar, mistakes when engaging the issues of 9/11, and, therefore, because I believe it is important not to leave unaddressed various problematic claims and assertions that have been made by Dr. Harris or Professor Chomsky concerning 9/11, I have tried to take the time that seemed to be necessary to be able to exercise due diligence with respect to a variety of issues that are commented on by Sam Harris and Noam Chomsky, and, as a result, from time to time, there is a certain repetition of material that emerges during the process of critically reflecting on their respective positions since, at certain points, their perspectives tend to overlap.

However, irrespective of whatever irritation a reader might feel as a result of the small amount of repetition that does occur in the following material, this should be measured against the mental anguish and turmoil that have been experienced by millions of innocent people in Iraq, Afghanistan, Libya, Yemen, Lebanon, and Syria whose lives have been lost, abused, tortured, wounded, displaced, mutilated and destroyed due to the fact, in part, that people such as Sam Harris and Noam Chomsky have failed to fulfill their responsibility and duty as intellectuals when it comes to the issue of 9/11 – namely, (1) "to insist upon the truth", and (2) "to see events in their historical perspective", and (3) to not disengage or detach themselves from events in a way that helps facilitate the very problems and tragedies that they claim to oppose. I'm sure that the individuals who have been most adversely affected by the events of 9/11 won't mind whatever relatively small amount of repetition occurs in the following pages because, unfortunately, such points need to be made again and again in order for those ideas and facts to have a chance of penetrating the shield of **<u>willful blindness</u>** that appears to engulf people such as Sam Harris and Noam Chomsky in the matter of 9/11.

Willful blindness is rooted in a legal principle – which actually has relevance to many non-legal contexts … including matters of science and research. This principle refers to instances in which a person can be held accountable for their actions if that individual could have known something or should have known something that substantively affects a given situation, but, instead, the person chooses not to act on, or take into account, what could have and should have been grasped so that appropriate actions might have been taken (for a more in depth exploration of the notion of willful blindness read Margaret Heffernan's book: *Willful Blindness: Why We Ignore the Obvious at Our Peril*).

]]

20

Peter Michael Ketchum and NIST

Consider the example of Peter Michael Ketchum. For much of his professional life, he was deeply ensconced in the world of high performance systems and scientific computation.

In 1997, he began working at NIST (The National Institute of Standards and Technology) which operates out of the Department of Commerce. From its inception, NIST has been tasked with engaging the processes through which industry sets standards and coordinating those activities with policies of the federal government.

Among other things, NIST attempts to help industry clarify the process of setting standards. In addition, NIST lends support to the foregoing process through a variety of activities, including research.

After a few years at NIST, Mr. Ketchum was assigned to the mathematical and computational sciences division of NIST. He also served as the chairperson for that division's seminar series in applied mathematics.

When, on August 21, 2002, NIST was placed in charge of investigating the cause of the complete destruction of three buildings at the World Trade Center on 9/11, Mr. Ketchum was not involved in either the research for, or writing of, various reports that were generated by NIST in conjunction with the foregoing investigation. However, he was aware that those activities were taking place.

For many years, Mr. Ketchum accepted the findings that had been recorded in a series of reports released by NIST that purported to account for the demise of the Twin Towers as well as the collapse of Building 7 on 9/11 that had been part of the World Trade Center in Manhattan. However, he had accepted the foregoing findings without really examining, or reflecting on, the contents of those reports because, during that period, he was of the general opinion that the work performed at NIST was of the highest caliber and that, as a general rule, its members conducted themselves with integrity when engaged in research.

In July of 2016, a friend mentioned to him that a certain amount of evidence was accumulating which seemed to suggest that the official position concerning 9/11 might not be the slam-dunk that the media and government had been claiming. The "official" position of the government consisted primarily of: (1) *The 9/11 Report: The National Commission on Terrorist Attacks Upon The United States*; (2) a series of reports released by NIST concerning the demise of buildings on 9/11 that occurred at the World Trade Center in New York, and (3) The Pentagon Performance Report that was issued in conjunction with the damage that was inflicted on the Pentagon on 9/11]

For approximately a month, Mr. Ketchum didn't follow up on the foregoing information. Eventually, he began to rigorously inquire into a variety of issues concerning 9/11, especially in relation to NIST's research efforts involving the destruction of buildings at the World Trade Center.   23

Within a relatively short period of time after initiating his own review of the NIST findings, Mr. Ketchum realized that NIST's account of what transpired on 9/11 at the World Trade Center was, to use his words on the matter, "not a sincere and genuine study." As a result, he became quite upset ... first, with himself, since, for sixteen years he really hadn't paid sufficiently close attention to an array of issues concerning 9/11, and, then, he became upset with NIST for the lack of integrity that characterized its reports concerning 9/11.

Once he was able to examine material concerning NIST's handling of its 9/11 investigation, Mr. Ketchum felt evidence overwhelmingly indicated that Buildings 1, 2 and 7 of the World Trade Center were brought down by controlled demolition rather than being due to a variety of structural damage that, supposedly had been caused by either crashing commercial jets and/or office fires that were initiated by spilled jet fuel or – in the case of Building 7 -- through just fires. Irrespective of the extent to which the aforementioned controlled demolition thesis might, or might not, be correct, Mr. Ketchum came to the conclusion that the NIST findings were not done in a competent manner and, therefore, were unacceptable.

Before moving on to explore some of the aspects of Mr. Ketchum's conceptual transformation concerning the events of 9/11, one might be prudent to consider some cautionary qualifications concerning the issue of controlled demolition in conjunction with the collapse of the Twin Towers and Building 7 at the World Trade Center on 9/11. More specifically, while there is ample evidence (some of which is presented in the present work) to indicate that multiple explosions occurred in different parts of the World Trade Center on 9/11, and while there is considerable evidence that can be cited (e.g., The Framing of 9/11, 2nd edition) in support of the claim that nano-thermite was present in dust samples from the World Trade Center, nevertheless, there are a number of facts that suggest something more exotic – but still not definitively identified -- also was taking place at the World Trade Center on 9/11 than just the use of explosives and nano-thermite with respect to the destruction of the World Trade Center on 9/11.

Thermite, thermate, and nano-thermite are not explosives. They are chemical compounds that, when ignited, are capable of burning their way through, among other things, metal objects (e.g., steel columns in a building), and, when properly orchestrated with explosives, form a system that is capable of sequentially removing sections of designated steel columns to bring about a controlled collapse of a building.

As indicated earlier, I do not dispute that both explosives and nano-thermite were present in, and utilized at, the World Trade Center in conjunction with the destruction of the two Twin Towers and Building 7 on 9/11. What I do dispute is that explosions and nano-thermite are not capable of accounting for certain phenomena that occurred in relation to the events at the World Trade Center on 9/11.

For example, If two 110 storey, 500, 000-ton buildings collapsed to the ground (whether through controlled demolition or through some sort of a conventional, progressive collapse that involved a pancaking of floors one on top of another), one would expect to find 220 stories of material on the ground. Yet, photographs of Ground Zero on the morning of 9/11 (one can see the not-yet destroyed Building 7 in the background) show that after the two towers had disappeared, there was not much more than piles, here and there, of 12 to 14 stories worth of steel on the ground.

Some people have argued that the reason why there is so little debris above ground at Ground Zero is because the weight of the "collapse" drove all that material down into the sub-basements. However, Dr. Wood has found "official" photographs demonstrating that the tunnels, rails, and cars for the Path Train that ran under the WTC showed only minor damage. Moreover, there was no debris from the towers down in the Path Train tunnels.

In addition, many of the stores in the concourse beneath the Twin Towers were not damaged. One of Dr. Wood's favorite photographs in this respect is a picture of a store in the concourse with a window full of famous Warner Brothers dolls – such as Bugs Bunny, Foghorn Leghorn, and the Road Runner – yet, the store (and this was true of many other stores) was not damaged.

Even more significantly, the World Trade Center was built over a section of concrete foundation that was poured over bedrock. The poured concrete is referred to as the 'bathtub' and it is intended to protect Lower Manhattan from being flooded by the Hudson River.

The bathtub-structure is, in some respects, fairly fragile. This was problematically demonstrated when some of the earth-moving equipment that had been brought in to help with the clean up process at Ground Zero were responsible for cracking the bathtub structure in a number of places.

Yet, one is led to believe that the collapse of 2, 110 storey, 500,000-ton buildings did not put even a scratch in that bathtub structure. Cranes weighing only a fraction of what the Twin Towers weighed could crack the bathtub structure, but the mammoth Twin Towers could not accomplish this. Surely, this is an anomaly that begs for critical reflection.

There is another problem surrounding the attempt to explain the destruction of the World Trade Towers either through a conventional progressive collapse due to fires or due to controlled explosions. More specifically, the seismic signal associated with the demise of the two towers was significantly less than one would expect to be associated with the 'collapse' of two such weighty buildings.

This was especially evident in the demise of the 47-storey Building 7. The destruction of this building had a seismic signal of .6 and was barely distinguishable from normal background noise for an average workday in Manhattan.

The seismic signal associated with the destruction of Building 1 was 2.3. The seismic signal for the demise of Building 2 was 2.1.

Those readings are comparable to the seismic reading associated with the Seattle Kingdom when it was brought down through controlled demolition. The difficulty here, however, is that the height and weight of the Twin Towers should have given expression – but did not -- to a potential energy that was some thirty times greater than the potential energy possessed by the Kingdome when the latter energy was released upon destruction.

There is an additional problem surrounding the length of the seismic signal according to Dr. Wood. For example, the length of the seismic signal for the South Tower's demise was about 8 seconds.

Most proponents of the controlled demolition idea with respect to the Twin Towers (and Building 7) often mention that all three buildings came down at close to free fall speeds. A conventional, progressive collapse (e.g., as in the pancake theory in which upper floors come crashing down on lower floors in a sequential manner) cannot be reconciled with such near free-fall speeds and would require much more time to crumble to the ground due to the resistance that each floor puts up before succumbing to the forces being exerted on those individual floors by the collapsing upper floors ... this is the principle of the conservation of momentum in action.

However, the idea of controlled demolition cannot account for why, say, the South Tower was destroyed at a rate that is faster than free fall. Yet, the roughly eight- second seismic signal associated with the destruction of the South and North Towers indicates that those events took less time than would have been the case if one dropped a bowling ball from the roof of the 110-storey structure unimpeded by air-resistance (approximately 9.5 seconds ... and factoring in air-resistance would slightly lengthen the duration of free fall for such an object).

Instances of controlled demolition approach near free fall velocities because buildings are rigged with cutter charges in such a way that the support columns are knocked out in a sequence that removes any resistance to the falling floors.

Consequently, in such cases, the time it takes for a designated building to come down is like dropping an object to the ground from the top of whatever building is being demolished through such controlled demolition.

For a building's destruction to register a seismic signal whose length indicates a time that is shorter than free-fall speeds suggests something is going on in that process of destruction other than controlled demolition. A seismic signal of such short duration might indicate that the building is not just falling freely through space (notwithstanding air-resistance) but is being propelled downward by some force.

On the other hand, a seismic signal of such short duration also might indicate that some kind of force had destroyed the building in such a way that eight, or so, seconds was all it took to register what was left of the building plus its contents with respect to impacting the ground. For example, if – for the sake of conversation – one were to hypothesize that some sort of force reduced a large number of floors to nothing more than dust and that such dust dispersed in a cloud over a large area, then the length of the seismic signal for such an event would be like dropping an object off a much shorter building, and, therefore, the time of free-fall would be much less than one would expect for a taller building.

During the press conference that marked the release of its initial, final report on Building 7, NIST indicated that the destruction of Building 7 was "whisper quiet". NIST – through its spokesperson, Shyam Sunder – used that description in conjunction with the demise of Building 7 in order to respond to a question about the possible use of explosives (in the form of controlled demolition) with respect to the destruction of Building 7.

Some might wish to argue that by saying what he did that Sunder was merely lying in order to try to hide evidence pointing to the presence of explosives and controlled demolition. However, by saying what he did about the fall of Building 7 being "whisper quiet", Sunder actually was undermining the position of NIST.

NIST claimed that Building 7 came down as a result of a progressive collapse that had been initiated through the way fire caused girders to expand and, in the process, generate torque forces on a key core beam and, thereby, led the beam to buckle. However, if Building 7 came down due to a progressive, pancake collapse, then, there should have been a lot of noise associated with such a collapse as one floor slammed into the next and, in addition, successive core beams and floor assemblies buckled and came apart.

However, if the demise of Building 7 was "whisper quiet", one is not talking about a conventional progressive collapse of the kind to which NIST subscribed. No noise, no conventional, progressive collapse.

By saying what he did in the press conference, Sunder is not only ruling out controlled demolition and explosions, he also is ruling out his own theory. So, if Building 7 came down "whisper quiet", then, one needs to find some other explanation for how that building came down.

In support of Sunder's "whisper quiet" comment, Dr. Wood indicates that some people were doing a video with Building 7 as a relatively distant backdrop. The building was coming down so silently that none of the participants realized what was going on until the building was already part way down.

A second point to consider in relation to the possible role of explosives or controlled demolition in bringing down three buildings at the World Trade Center revolves around the following anomaly. On five different occasions the Earth's magnetic field shifted during 9/11.

The times of these abrupt shifts in the magnetic field correspond very closely with five events at the World Trade Center. The first shift in Earth's magnetic field occurred precisely at the time when whatever struck the North Tower created a hole in that building. A second shift in the magnetic field took place at the exact time when the South Tower was impacted by something ... most people believe a commercial jet was implicated with respect to the holes in the Twin Towers. Three further shifts in the magnetic field happened at the precise time that Building 1, Building 2, and Building 7 came down.

Controlled demolitions could not have caused such shifts in the Earth's magnetic field. Conventional progressive collapses cannot account for such abrupt shifts either.

The shifts in the Earth's magnetic field were recorded through the magnetometer site in Alaska. The site consists of a number of different stations, and the shift recordings were drawn from six of those stations.

In each of the foregoing cases, the magnetometer indicated that for a period of time the magnetic field signal started going down prior to a given event at the World Trace Center (i.e., being struck by something or coming down). When the five aforementioned events took place, the magnetic field signal began to rise again.

Of course, one might wish to argue that the correlation between the two sets of data – one set in Alaska involving magnetic field readings and one set in New York involving three, steel-framed, high-rise buildings – was purely coincidental. And, if such a correlation occurred with respect to just one of the five events in New York, but not in the other four, a person might be inclined to accept such a possibility, but when the abrupt shifts in the magnetic field occur on five different occasions and are tied to specific times at which events in New York transpired, then one might be wise to start looking for some other explanation.

There are a number of other anomalous phenomena associated with the events of 9/11 that occurred at the World Trade Center which tend to indicate that something more than explosives and nano-thermite were involved in the destruction of the World Trade Center buildings on 9/11. One can learn more about those additional phenomena by reading Dr. Wood's book *Where Did The Towers Go?*, but the foregoing several pages of commentary should be enough to help engender a certain amount of caution in the reader with respect to keeping an open mind about what might have transpired at the World Trade Center on 9/11 ... we now return you to our regularly scheduled program concerning Peter Michael Ketchum.

One of the many factors that bothered Mr. Ketchum about the NIST reports was that they failed to exhibit due diligence with respect to determining whether, or not, there was any evidence that explosives of one kind or another might have been present at the World Trade Center on 9/11. For instance in a public statement (carried on C-Span) Dr. Shyam Sunder (Director of the NIST Building and Fire Research Laboratory) announced that before stating what NIST had found to be the cause for the collapse of Building 7, he wanted to state what NIST had not discovered in its investigations ... which was that NIST had not found any evidence indicating that explosives of any kind had been involved in the collapse of Building 7.

34

Dr. Sunder stated that the size of the blast necessary to bring down Building 7 would have had a very loud sound associated with it yet <u>none</u> of the video examined by the researchers concerning Building 7 provided evidence that such a blast had taken place. Furthermore, NIST had not discovered any witnesses who reported hearing such a blast.

Nevertheless, Barry Jennings -- who was serving as the Deputy Director of the Emergency Services Department for the New York City Housing Authority on 9/11 – had given public statements (independently corroborated, at least in part, by Michael Hess) indicating that as Mr. Jennings and Mr. Hess were descending the stairs of Building 7 (because the elevators were not working), the structure was rocked by an explosion from below (which occurred prior to the demise of Buildings 1 and 2) that took out the 6th floor landing near which he had been standing, and, as a result, he and Mr. Hess were forced to retreat back up the stairwell and seek an alternative exit from the building.

Furthermore, when the two individuals were finally rescued and led down to the lobby area of Building 7, Mr. Jennings described the entire ground floor as being in total ruins. Earlier, on his way to the Emergency Command Center located on the 23rd floor of Building 7, he had gone through that same lobby area and it had been in pristine, undamaged condition.

35

In addition, William Rodriguez, Kenny Johannemann, Jose Sanchez, Salvatore Giambanco, Anthony Satalamacchia (all of whom worked at the Twin Towers), along with Felipe David (an employee of a company that serviced the candy machines in the Twin Towers) and, perhaps, <u>sixteen</u> other individuals, all experienced massive explosions that took place in the basement complex of the North tower of the World Trade Center <u>prior</u> to anything striking the building above. Moreover, John Schroeder, a New York City fire fighter, also reported being bounced around on 9/11 as if he were in a pinball machine when a series of explosions rocked the North tower he was in – explosions that occurred prior to the demise of the South Tower -- and as he evacuated the former building, he discovered that the lobby area – including 2-3 inch glass windows and marble-covered surfaces -- had been completely destroyed by one, or more, explosions.

Yet, NIST did not bother to interview any of the individuals mentioned in the last paragraph, nor did they talk with the aforementioned Barry Jennings, in relation to the possibility that explosions had occurring at the World Trade Center on 9/11. Therefore, notwithstanding the claims of Shyam Sunder to the contrary, apparently, NIST did not look very hard to uncover evidence concerning possible explosions that might be related to the demise of Buildings 1, 2, or 7 on 9/11 ... and, indeed, when one does not look for evidence of explosions, then declaring that no such evidence has been found becomes quite easy.

NIST proclaimed – through the voice of Dr. Sunder – that researchers had: "... identified thermal expansion as a new phenomenon that can cause the collapse of a structure. For the first time we have shown that fire can induce a progressive collapse."

However, when Peter Ketchum, a former NIST employee, critically examined the evidence that NIST put forward in support of the foregoing claim, Mr. Ketchum stated: "The explanation that is given by NIST for the collapse of Building 7 sounds like a Rube Goldberg Device" in which an overly complex, fantastic, and irrelevant explanation is used to try to account for something that can be explained in a much simpler manner.

According to Dr. Sunder, NIST had identified column 79 as the weak link that was the first column to buckle and, in turn, led to the successive failures of other columns. Yet, as Mr. Ketchum has indicated in a public statement concerning the foregoing matter, the position of the column (located off-center) that allegedly buckled and supposedly initiated the collapse of Building 7 should have led to an asymmetrical collapse of the building, but, instead, the building came straight down in a symmetrical fashion, collapsing into its own footprint rather than asymmetrically tipping over in some fashion and, as a result, spilling over into adjoining areas on the ground below.

Consequently, Mr. Ketchum referred to NIST's account of the collapse as being "just fantasy land," He added that: "Asymmetric damage does not lead to symmetric collapse," and, furthermore: "It's very difficult to get a building to collapse symmetrically."

Moreover, Mr. Ketchum notes that when one takes the computer model NIST constructed in an attempt to demonstrate the nature of the alleged collapse process and compares that model with actual video footage of the demise of Building 7, the two do not resemble one another. In fact, the NIST computer model of Building 7 never actually takes one through the entire collapse process, but, instead, stops with the buckling of column 79 and, then, <u>assumes</u> that everything else that follows took place in a way that is depicted by actual video footage of events on 9/11.

Shyam Sunder claims that – with absolutely no evidence to back up his assertion – NIST's structural model of the collapse "...matches quite well with a video of the event." Apparently, he believes that as long as one asserts something with sufficient confidence, then this will be enough to make whatever one says true even if such a statement is at odds with an array of facts.

Peter Ketchum mentions that he remembers seeing a statement from NIST indicating that the researchers were having difficulty trying to figure out why Building 7 collapsed. In fact, earlier during its investigation, NIST researchers proposed a theory concerning the collapse of Building 7 that subsequently had to be discarded as untenable.

38

Eventually, they resolved their difficulty by fabricating a fictional, fantastical account concerning the collapse of Building 7. Even, then, they were forced to amend that second theory and acknowledge the validity of the arguments of David Chandler, a high school physics teacher in New York, which demonstrated that Building 7 was in free fall for at least three seconds ... a fact that is entirely at odds with the notion of a progressive collapse in which floors successively slam into the floors below them and, therefore, at no point do those floors have an opportunity to exhibit free-fall behavior.

The NIST computer models of the progressive collapse that, supposedly, enveloped Building 1 (North) and Building 2 (South) of the World Trade Center commits the same error as NIST did in conjunction with its model of the Building 7 collapse. In other words, in the case of each of the foregoing three buildings, the NIST models only take things up to the point at which collapses supposedly were initiated and does not provide any of the details concerning how such a collapse, once it was initiated, would proceed in a way that is capable of being verified by what had been recorded with video on 9/11.

When Dr. John Gross – at the time, a senior researcher for NIST -- was asked about whether NIST had been tasked with the responsibility for determining the cause of the collapses of World Trade Center buildings on 9/11, Dr. Gross responded by saying:

"We found ... what happened I think ... we've scientifically demonstrated what was required to initiate the collapse. Once the collapse initiated, the video evidence was rather clear ... it was not stopped by the floors below, so, there was no calculation that we did to determine that ... what was clear on the video."

Notwithstanding Dr. Gross's foregoing comments, neither he nor NIST have scientifically demonstrated that the collapse scenario they advanced could account for the properties of the collapses that were captured by video, and, in fact, Dr. Gross admits as much when he acknowledges that NIST did not perform any calculations to demonstrate that their model would be compatible with the video evidence, and, instead, merely assumed their conclusions by claiming -- without evidence – that the video evidence confirmed their model.

Peter Ketchum – the former NIST employee who belatedly became aware of the incredibly shoddy work perpetrated by NIST in relation to its investigation into the collapse of three buildings at the World Trade Center on 9/11 – also has commented on the properties of the rubble that remained following the collapse of the two 110-storey towers plus the 47-storey Building 7. He indicates that there was virtually nothing left to the buildings ... that almost everything had been reduced to a powdered state.

Joe Casaliggi, a New York City fire fighter, recalls going through the rubble at Ground Zero following 9/11. He notes:

"You have two 110 storey office buildings. You don't find a desk. You don't find a chair ... you don't find a telephone ... a computer ... the biggest part of a telephone that I found was half of the key pad ... and it was about this big [spreading his thumb and forefinger apart a few inches]. The building collapsed in dust."

Dr. Steven Levin, an environmental medical doctor working at Mt. Sinai Hospital in New York, went through a list of some of the destruction that transpired at the World Trade Center. He said:

"We're talking here of 43,600 windows, 600,000 square feet of glass [Note: Much of which is several inches thick], 200,000 tons of structural steel, 5 million square feet of gypsum, 6 acres of marble, and 425,000 cubic yards of concrete turned, in good part, to a cloud. ... I was astonished at the degree to which solid materials were turned into pulverized dust as a consequence of that building collapse."

However, as Mr. Ketchum was alluding to earlier, the foregoing degree of destruction is inconsistent with the idea of a progressive collapse of buildings at the World Trade Center. Indeed, Dr. Judy Wood, a former professor of engineering mechanics, indicates that if there had been three progressive collapses that took place at the World Trade Center on 9/11, then, one would expect to find roughly 267-stories worth of materials at Ground Zero, and, instead, one finds only three piles of rubble, none of which is more than 12-14 stories high ... a problem that is captured in the title of her 2010 book: *Where Did The Towers Go?*

Mr. Ketchum also notes another inconsistency in the NIST theory of a progressive collapse involving Buildings 1 and 2 on 9/11. More specifically, a progressive collapse is driven by gravity, and, therefore, the force of a gravitational collapse is directed downward. Yet, on 9/11, video evidence reveals that there were multi-ton sections of steel perimeter columns that were being projected hundreds of feet in a horizontal direction.

The force of gravity cannot explain such lateral movement. Gravity operates in a downward vertical direction, not horizontally, and consequently, NIST failed to identify the source of the force that was propelling multi-ton steel beams in a sideways direction.

Another set of facts that is inconsistent with the notion that the three buildings at the World Trade Center underwent a progressive collapse as a result of damage from commercial jet crashes and/or office fires has to do with the temperatures that, for months, were recorded at Ground Zero following 9/11 despite the fact that the piles of rubble had been sprayed with thousands of gallons of water. NIST reported that the maximum temperatures reached within the World Trade Center buildings were approximately 480 degrees Fahrenheit or 250 degrees Celsius.

For instance, despite the fact that substantial rain fell at Ground Zero on the 14th of September, thermographic imaging directed at the base of the three destroyed buildings at the World Trade Center detected some hot spots associated with those buildings that registered temperatures in excess of 1,300 degrees Fahrenheit, while several additional hot spots exhibited temperatures of over a thousand degrees Fahrenheit.

The U.S. Department of Labor stated on its "A Dangerous Workplace' web page that:

"Underground fires burned at temperatures up to 2,000 degrees (Fahrenheit)."

Furthermore, the October 2012 issue of *Professional Safety* – the journal of the American Society of Safety Engineers – contained the following words concerning the issue of temperatures at Ground Zero following 9/11:

"Thermal measurements taken by helicopter each day showed underground temperatures ranging from 400 degrees Fahrenheit to more than 2,800 degrees Fahrenheit."

A December 2001 History Channel program called "Rise and Fall of the Towers" indicated that: "As recently as the end of November, it was still 1,100 degrees down underneath the rubble." During December, ice would form on the rubble pile early in the day, but beneath the surface, the ground was still smoldering and one person working on the pile observed that the ground wasn't frozen but "kind of bubbled underneath your feet."

The observable fires that were present in the underground areas of the World Trade Center were finally extinguished on December 19, 2001, more than three months after 9/11. Yet, the burning question of what was the source of those fires has not been successfully extinguished.

Some people theorized that the source of the fuel for the fires came from the gasoline in the cars that were parked beneath the World Trade Center.

The American Society of Safety Engineers stated in its aforementioned journal that nearly 2,000 cars were located that had been parked on three underground floors of the Center, and although some of those vehicles had exploded and were completely burned, many other cars were in drivable condition – neither crushed nor burned. Moreover, the journal article indicated that "... gasoline in a car either explodes or it remains inside the tank ... it does not leak out and go looking for fires to be fueled."

The Society of Safety Engineers also indicated that a tank containing 72,000 gallons of fuel that was stored in the basement of the World Trade Center had been discovered. Although the tank was slightly damaged, no leaks were detected in the tank, and the fuel in the tank was removed.

Most of the office equipment in the buildings had – somehow – been transformed into dust on 9/11, and, therefore, could not serve as a source of fuel, and, moreover, there were many stores in the underground shopping complex that were still intact and their contents never burned. So, if 2,000 parked cars, a huge fuel storage tank, office equipment, and subterranean stores were not fueling the high temperatures at Ground Zero that continued for months on end, what was responsible for that phenomenon?

The television program "Relics from the Ruins" that aired on the History Channel featured an eight ton I-beam taken from Ground Zero that was six

44

inches thick and bent in the shape of a horseshoe. A worker commented on the I-beam and said:

"I found it hard to believe that it actually bent because of the size of it and how there's no cracks in the iron. It bent without almost a single crack in it. It takes thousands of degrees to bend steel like this,"

--Note: Steel melts at 2,800 degrees Fahrenheit – 1,500 degrees Celsius – and softens at 1,100 degrees Fahrenheit 593 degrees Celsius ... for steel to melt or bend in the foregoing manner usually requires that the temperature to which steel is exposed be sustained for a period of time --

and yet, as previously noted, NIST insisted that the maximum temperature attained by fires at the World Trade Center was about 480 degrees Fahrenheit.

Some people have maintained that traces of a substance were discovered at Ground Zero and that, upon analysis, the material was identified to be the incendiary/explosive known as nano-thermite. When nano-thermite is ignited it burns at around 4,800 degrees Fahrenheit and since its chemical composition provides it with its own source of oxygen, it is capable of burning in conditions that are devoid of oxygen (such as underwater).

Whether nano-thermite was the fuel that maintained the high-temperature at Ground Zero going for months or was responsible for bending an eight ton Steel I-beam into a horseshoe shape is unknown ... and for those who wish to claim that nano-thermite might have been the fuel that subsidized the more than three months worth of high-temperatures that were recorded at the World Trade Center following 9/11, then, as a homework assignment, you might try to calculate how much nano-thermite would be necessary to sustain such a persistent set of high temperatures for that length of period of time. In any event, what is clear is that there is no known way through which military grade nano-thermite could form naturally in the dust at Ground Zero, and, therefore, its presence there needs to be explained.

NIST refused to look – at least in any manner that can be called scientific – for evidence that explosives had been present at the World Trade Center on 9/11, and it did not choose to investigate whether, or not, the high temperatures that, for months, had been discovered to be present at Ground Zero following the events of 9/11 might have had anything to do with the collapse of three steel-structure buildings on 9/11. In fact, as Peter Ketchum noted in his public statement concerning the matter, NIST seemed to do everything it could to avoid looking for evidence that might indicate the presence of explosives at Ground Zero on 9/11.

According to Dr. Sunder, "We conducted the study without bias, without interference from anyone, and dedicated ourselves to do the very best job we could. And, in fact, I would suggest that the public should ... at this point recognize that science is really behind what we say." Actual facts belie the foregoing assertion.

The only kind of science that is behind the NIST reports concerning 9/11 is the sort of research that cannot but induce Americans to distance themselves from such so-called scientific activity and become "unscientific" in the best sense of the latter term. In other words, the sort of research conducted by NIST in conjunction with 9/11 is the kind of process that forces one to conclude that such "scientists" can no longer be considered to be honest brokers of truth, and if the NIST manner of research – as exemplified in relation to 9/11 -- is "scientific", then, one needs to become "unscientific" so that evidence, objectivity, rigor, love of the truth, and integrity once again matter.

Peter Ketchum – a scientist – did not investigate the events of 9/11 for nearly sixteen years. He merely accepted the word of others ... until a friend's casual remark induced him to look into the matter more carefully.

As far as the issue of 9/11 is concerned, Mr. Ketchum didn't really begin to become an honest broker of the truth concerning those events until he actually begin to look at relevant evidence some 16 years after the events of 9/11 had taken place. He became an objective, honest broker of the truth in relation to 9/11 when he made the requisite efforts to acquire insight into the nature of 9/11 in a manner that was rooted in a rigorous process that was transparent, open, not intended to evade difficult problems, or mislead and distort (through commission or omission) with respect to relevant issues, as well as be critically and fairly responsive to actual evidence rather than be ruled by propaganda, indoctrination, and forces of undue influence in relation to the issue of 9/11.

Having done the foregoing does not mean that his conclusions concerning 9/11 are necessarily correct or true. Nonetheless, he has done, and is doing, what any objective and honest broker of the truth must do in order to try to gain insight into the nature of truth with respect to some given issue … in this case 9/11.

Unfortunately, there are many other scientists who continue to fail to examine the actual evidence concerning 9/11 and, as a result, remain in ignorance or in denial concerning the nature of the events of 9/11. Sam Harris is one such scientist.

Sam Harris and 9/11

Dr. Harris is a neuroscientist. Or, perhaps, more to the point as far as the present discussion is concerned, he was trained in sciences exploring the brain, and, therefore, is familiar with the methods and processes of science.

Yet, interestingly enough, I have not come across any statements in his books (and I've read three of those works), nor have I encountered any statements in several podcasts and interviews he has given, that touch on the subject of 9/11 which provide any indication that he actually has looked at evidence concerning 9/11. Instead, almost everything he has to say on the subject is in response to various conspiratorial claims that certain people have made about whom they believe is responsible for 9/11 and with whom Dr. Harris wishes to take issue.

In what follows, I will provide the text for a number of lengthy statements that have been made by Dr. Harris concerning 9/11. As I believe will soon become fairly evident, those statements encompass a litany of problems that seem to be devoid of any quality of scientific or even rational analysis.

For instance, during a recorded conversation between Steven Wright and Sam Harris that appeared on SamHarris.org and which tried to respond to various issues concerning 9/11, Dr. Harris states:

"When you follow each one of these anomalies to some alternative conclusion ... it's never the same conclusion. There's no unified view of what would explain everything that happened here. There's dozens or hundreds or more different things all of which are mutually incompatible but all of which are different from the prevailing story that Al-Qaeda did it. But, there is no unified view that makes it the perfect work of evil genius to have George Bush sitting reading 'My Pet Goat' when this thing goes off. Now, what evil genius decided to do it that way?

"I mean there's larger phenomenon of conspiracy thinking which again, once you connect it to the fake news phenomenon that we're living through now, it becomes hugely consequential. It's like I've always thought of conspiracy thinking as a kind of pornography of doubt. There's an itch that people are scratching here. People who, for the most part, feel disempowered and imagine that people in power are always doing something malicious and that whenever you can explain something based on incompetence, it's never really incompetence. The irony here is that they are attributing a super human level of competence to people where there's never any evidence of this kind of competence.

"Bill Clinton couldn't stop a semen-stained dress from appearing on the evening news. Presidents can't do these sorts of things, and, yet, we are asked to imagine that thousands upon thousands of psychopathic collaborators killed some of the most productive people in our society in downtown Manhattan ... just for what? The pleasure of sending us to war in the Middle East ... not to Saudi Arabia where the hijackers came from ... but to Iraq when we could easily have found a pretext to go to war anyway and what a great war that was, and, yet, they did this without a single leak ... there's not one person with a guilty conscience who got on 60 minutes and spilled the beans ... and, yet, generally speaking, you can't even keep the next iPhone from being left on the bar before it gets released. It's an amazing double-standard of reasonableness that gives us this kind of thinking."

Although Dr. Harris mentions the issue of 9/11 anomalies toward the beginning of his foregoing statement, he never specifies what sorts of anomalies he has in mind. Consequently, one has no concrete context upon which to reflect in order to determine whether what he is saying is true or not.

Furthermore, when he speaks about following each one of the foregoing sorts of anomalies – whatever they might be -- to some alternative conclusion, once again, his statement lacks specificity. We don't know which alternative conclusions he is alluding to or what he, or anyone else, considers the nature of the relationship to be, if any, between various anomalies and various conclusions.

All we have is his declarative statement that is embedded in a context of vagueness. He proceeds to complain that "there's no unified view of what would explain everything that happened here," but he doesn't offer any concrete evidence to substantiate what he claims ... all he offers is unsubstantiated assertion.

Dr. Harris maintains there is "no unified view of what would explain everything that happened here." However, given that the so-called "prevailing view that al-Qaeda did it" also fails to explain everything that happened on 9/11 – in fact fails to explain in a factual manner nearly all the events of 9/11 -- Dr. Harris never explains why there should be an alternative, unified view that is capable of explaining everything among those who do not accept the "prevailing story that al-Qaeda did it" since the so-called prevailing view is, itself, unable to provide such a unified account.

Be this as it may, nonetheless, contrary to the foregoing claim of Dr. Harris, <u>the one thing on which all those who reject the "prevailing story" agree</u> – a point that Dr. Harris entirely ignores – is that the "prevailing story that al-Qaeda did it" suffers from a variety of problems. Moreover, those many problems begin with the fact that at least 6-7 of the alleged 9/11 hijackers – all of whom, supposedly, perished in the four plane crashes that occurred on 9/11 -- were confirmed as still being alive by a post-9/11 BBC news item.

Did some people jump to conclusions concerning 9/11 or about who might have been responsible for perpetrating that tragedy before they carefully examined all of the evidence? Yes, they did, and Sam Harris is one of those individuals?

In his foregoing statement, Dr. Harris contends that in relation to various claims concerning the nature of 9/11: "There's dozens or hundreds, or more, different things all of which are mutually incompatible but all of which are different from the prevailing story that Al-Qaeda did it." However, since Dr. Harris doesn't specify what the nature of the alleged incompatibilities are, we have no evidential basis for determining whether, or not, his assertion is correct or whether, or not, such alleged incompatibilities might, through one means or another, be capable of being reconciled in some fashion.

In the previously quoted excerpt, Dr. Harris mentions the idea of a prevailing story – namely, that al-Qaeda is responsible for the events of 9/11 – but what is that story based on? As I believe has been demonstrated in my own books (namely, *The Essence of September 11th, 2nd Edition* and *Framing 9/11, 2nd Edition*), and as Judy Wood has pointed out -- with considerable detail -- in her book: *Where Did The Towers Go?*, and as David Ray Griffin argued in books such as The *9/11 Commission*

Report: Omissions and Distortions, and as Webster Tarpley expounded in his book: *9/11: Synthetic Terror*, and as Rebekah Roth has established in her "*Methodical*" trilogy, the "prevailing story that al-Qaeda did it" is untenable at nearly every – if not every – juncture.

As has been demonstrated in the foregoing books, there are substantial problems with *The 9/11 Commission Report*, *The Pentagon Performance Report*, various NIST reports, and a variety of reports from the FBI. So, why should anyone accept the prevailing story that al-Qaeda did it as being the indisputable, definitive treatment of 9/11?

The whole "prevailing story" notion seems to give expression to little more than an argument from authority in which one is supposed to accept such a story just because individuals in authority have told it. Unfortunately, despite being filled with lots of information (much of it amounting to little more than misinformation and disinformation), the "prevailing story" is almost entirely devoid of any relevant facts concerning the events of 9/11.

What evidence is there that is capable of proving – independently of the government's framing of the story -- that al-Qaeda carried out the attacks on 9/11. In point of fact, there is absolutely zero reliable evidence indicating that al-Qaeda carried out – or was capable of carrying out – the events of 9/11.

The FBI, itself (both through its website as well as through it's, then, director, Robert Mueller) admitted there was no evidence tying 'Usama bin Laden to the events of 9/11. Furthermore, the confessions of Khalid Sheikh Mohammed that implicated bin Laden, Mohammed Atta and others – and were obtained thorough nearly 200 rounds of water-boarding -- have never been confirmed by independent sources (and the similar confessions of other individuals that were induced through torture do not constitute independent confirmation), nor have those "confessions" ever been subjected to rigorous cross examination (indeed, the CIA prevented the members of the 9/11 Commission from having any contact with those who were 'confessing' to the crimes of 9/11).

Moreover, contrary to the aforementioned contentions of Dr. Harris, why should one assume that George Bush's reading of 'My Pet Goat' had anything to do with the plan for 9/11 or that such a reading was put in play by some evil genius? In order to determine whether, or not, George Bush was culpable in relation to 9/11, a proper investigation of those events must be permitted. [And, by "proper", I mean an investigation that is: Independent – i.e., not run by the government; fully funded (rather than being substantially underfunded as the 9/11 Commission had been); provided with subpoena power, and requiring sworn testimony -- unlike the 9/11 Commission testimony of Bush,

Cheney and others -- with penalties of perjury or worse for knowingly offering false statements].

Sam Harris's foregoing, extended statement is indulging in a form of argument in which he gets to supply all of the premises against which he wishes to argue. Yet, the premises of his argument have nothing to do with a central issue – namely, whether, or not, the "prevailing story" that Dr. Harris is unjustifiably treating as the default perspective concerning 9/11 is capable of successfully being defended when it is rigorously examined … something that Dr. Harris has provided no indication of having done (either with respect to defending or examining).

The words "a kind of pornography of doubt" that Dr. Harris advances in conjunction with his criticism of conspiracy theories constitutes a nice turn of phrase, but, what does it actually mean and how relevant is it? On any given day, in numerous courtrooms, in virtually every state in America, as well as in a variety of Federal courts, there are numerous conspiracies that have proven to be true.

Consequently, Dr. Harris needs to clarify what he means by the phrase "a kind of pornography of doubt" in conjunction with conspiracy theories that have been proven to be true on a regular basis in the courtrooms of America. As it stands, the phrase "a kind of pornography of doubt" seems to be little more than an attempt to cast aspersions upon anyone who has the temerity to question or harbor doubts concerning the viability of the "official" story concerning 9/11.

Dr, Harris refers, in a pejorative fashion, to the itch that people supposedly are scratching with respect to 9/11 (i.e., and such an itch is described by Dr. Harris as being nothing more than a matter of individuals feeling disempowered and who "imagine that people in power are always doing something malicious"). However, he apparently fails to consider the possibility that the underlying motivation of the individuals to whom he is alluding might have to do, instead, with not being satisfied with the "prevailing story" concerning 9/11.

Maybe such individuals are "merely" trying to seek truth and justice in relation to the events of 9/11, as well as attempting to save the country from the ruinous ramifications of the government-sponsored and media-sponsored malignancy that has enveloped the issue of 9/11. In other words, perhaps the individuals that Dr. Harris wishes to malign are not necessarily motivated by an ideology of false imagination or a thirst for conspiracy as he claims is the case.

Doesn't this kind of search for truth, justice, and a way to protect the country describe what is going on – at least to some extent -- in a courtroom when a prosecutor charges someone with conspiracy to commit various crimes? Moreover, couldn't those who do not accept the "official" story concerning 9/11 be motivated by similar goals?

Furthermore, what is one to make of the conspiracy thinking that is at the heart of the "prevailing story" – i.e., that al-Qaeda perpetrated 9/11? The mother of all conspiracy theories is that 19 Arab hijackers conspired with a guy in a cave in Afghanistan – namely, 'Usama bin Laden -- to perpetrate 9/11, and, therefore, if Harris's foregoing turn of phrase – i.e., "a kind of pornography of doubt" -- is to have substantive value, then, presumably, the "pornography of doubt" that Dr. Harris believes stains conspiracy thinking must also be applicable to his own conspiracy theory – namely, the one that is at the heart of the "prevailing story" ... that 20 Arabs conspired to attack America on 9/11?

In his foregoing extended statement, Dr Harris tries to suggest that the itch being scratched in conjunction with 9/11 is nothing more than a matter of: "People who, for the most part, feel disempowered and imagine that people in power are always doing something malicious and that whenever you can explain something based on incompetence, it's never really incompetence" Where is (or what is) the proof that justifies such an assertion?

At best, Dr. Harris offers vague sorts of anecdotal references in support of his position. At no point, however, does he engage in a serious analysis of actual evidence concerning 9/11.

He always operates at a meta-level. In other words, he only addresses conspiracy theories concerning the events of 9/11, and, as a result, he never actually explores real evidence concerning the events of that day.

In addition, Dr. Harris tries to give the impression that the events of 9/11 can be adequately explained by the issue of "incompetence" rather than having to refer to any kind of conspiracy, but what is the nature of the evidence that the events of 9/11 can all be explained by the notion of "incompetence"? What are the specific facts and arguments that demonstrate that everything that went on prior to, during, and following 9/11 were all a function of incompetence?

Dr. Harris says there is never any evidence of the kind of competence to which he claims that conspiracy thinking is alluding. However, since he is entirely vague at this juncture concerning what, specifically, he means by such statements, one has nothing on which to base an assessment of whether he is right, or not, concerning his claims in this regard.

Moreover, notwithstanding the fact that Dr. Harris seems to believe that Bill Clinton's inability to prevent the release of evidence concerning a semen-stained dress indicates that presidents are powerless to prevent leaks from occurring that will expose their high crimes and misdemeanors, nevertheless, his Clinton example actually undermines Dr. Harris's perspective concerning the issue of leaks rather than substantiates that point of view. More specifically, Robert Wright, Jr., Sibel Edmonds, Colonel Anthony Schafer, and Coleen Rowley all attempted to leak information to the public about various governmental anomalies concerning 9/11 but were either ignored, censored, or placed under a gag order, and, as a result, Dr. Harris's use of the Bill Clinton example tends to disprove the point that Dr. Harris seems to be trying to make rather than demonstrate it.

Dr. Harris also overlooks – or is ignorant about – what happened to an FAA employee – James P. Hopkins -- who discovered information (which ran counter to the "official" story) that he considered to be relevant to the investigation of 9/11 and tried to forward the information up the chain of command. He was fired for his efforts in that regard.

That individual fought to get his job back. Eventually, he won his case, but, subsequently, was killed during a car accident in Washington, D.C.

Dr. Harris also ignores – or is ignorant of – articles that appeared on May 7, 2004 in both the *New York Times* and *Chicago Sun-Times* that referred to a meeting of 16 air traffic controllers that took place before noon on the morning of September 11th, 2001 at the New York Air Route Traffic Control Center in Ronkonkoma, New York. The air traffic controllers met in a conference room in the basement -- known as the "Bat Cave" -- and passed around a microphone so that each of the individuals could share, in a recorded fashion, his, her, or their recollections and impressions concerning the events of 9/11.

<u>Several months later</u> those tapes were destroyed by a quality assurance manager at the aforementioned Ronkonkoma center. The destruction took place despite the fact that <u>three days after the events of 9/11</u>, the FAA had sent out an order to all departments – including the one for which the foregoing quality assurance manager worked -- indicating that personnel were to "retain and secure until further notice ALL Administrative/Operational data and records" concerning the events of 9/11.

When asked why he destroyed the tapes, the quality assurance manager stipulated that he felt the flight controllers were not in a state of mind that would have enabled them to have voluntarily consented to making such statements. However, he provided no evidence to back up the foregoing claim, nor was he qualified to make such a determination, and, most importantly of all, he was in violation of the aforementioned directive that had been issued by the FAA several months before he destroyed the tapes.

When the quality assurance manager destroyed the recording that had been made by the 16 flight controllers, he is reported to have crushed the tapes in his hand and, then, cut the tape into little pieces, and, finally, deposited the cut up tape in various trash receptacles that were located in different parts of the building. Given the lengths to which the aforementioned quality assurance manager went in order to destroy the testimony of 16 air traffic controllers concerning the events of 9/11, one can't help but wonder about the nature of the contents of those recordings.

At this point, one might also re-introduce, the aforementioned public statement given by Barry Jennings, the Deputy Director of the Emergency Services Department for the New York City Housing Authority on 9/11, concerning his experience in Building 7 in relation to the occurrence of explosions on 9/11 at the World Trade Center. His account -- along with evidence from many members of the New York City fire and police departments -- was also ignored by the 9/11 Commission.

Or consider the case of David Schippers -- who might best be known to some people as the lead investigative and prosecuting counsel for the House of Representative's impeachment proceedings against William Jefferson Clinton. In an October 13, 2001 story run by the *Indianapolis Star* one discovers that nearly a month and a half prior to 9/11, he [Mr. Schippers] had spoken with several FBI agents who were hoping for some legal advice.

The article describes how the two agents disclosed that they had reliable information specifying how lower Manhattan was to be a target in a terrorist attack that would involve the use of hijacked airplanes as weapons. The information they had included targets, dates, and funding pathways.

The reason for their speaking with Mr. Schippers is that they both had been removed from the investigation and had been threatened with being prosecuted under the National Security Act if they spoke out about what they knew. According to the two FBI agents, the threats and obstruction apparently came from FBI headquarters in Washington.

During the interview, Mr. Schippers claimed that some six weeks or so prior to 9/11, he had tried without success on a number of occasions, to get in touch with Attorney General Ashcroft in order to pass on the information that Mr. Schippers had learned through the two FBI agents. The Attorney General did not return any of Mr. Schippers' calls to the former's office.

Finally, one of the friends of the Attorney General who had been contacted by Mr. Schippers in relation to FBI information got back in touch with the Chicago lawyer (i.e., David Schippers). The friend of the Attorney General said that John Ashcroft had received the information and would call Mr. Schippers the next day.

The next day Mr. Schippers did receive a call but not from the Attorney General. According to Mr. Schippers, someone else, calling on behalf of the Attorney General, said that the matter would be investigated, and following that investigation, Mr. Schippers would be informed of what had been discovered and/or done.

Mr. Schippers passed on his information to the Attorney General approximately a month before the events of 9/11. Nonetheless, as of the October 2001 interview date, Mr. Schippers had not been contacted by the Attorney General with respect to the very detailed information concerning the September 11, 2001 attacks.

Finally, one shouldn't forget – as appears to be the case with Dr. Harris (or, perhaps, he never knew) -- that more than twelve individuals (a number of them worked for the Pentagon, some as members of the Pentagon police) came forward after 9/11 and indicated that just prior to the explosions which occurred at that complex on the morning of September 11, 2001, the <u>only</u> plane they saw approach the Pentagon flew on the <u>north side of the Citgo gas station</u> that was located approximately a mile, or so, from the Pentagon. This is a crucial issue because *The Pentagon Performance Report* indicates that the plane that supposedly struck the Pentagon had a flight path that <u>proceeded along a line to the south of that Citgo station</u> and that, among other things, took the craft over a Virginia Department of Transportation communication antenna.

If the testimony of the foregoing 12 individuals is correct, then, the findings of *The Pentagon Performance Report* are brought into serious question because the only plane that was near to the Pentagon at the time of the explosions would have struck (if it struck) the Pentagon at an angle that is entirely at odds with the "official story." Moreover, many commercial and military pilots have indicated that the south-side flight line that is promoted by the official story would have involved unmanageable g-forces (as well as a substantial destabilizing "ground effect") in order for American Airlines Flight 77 to be able to avoid the aforementioned Virginia Department of Transportation antenna and still be able to skim over the grass on the Pentagon lawn and, then, enter the Pentagon on the level of the ground floor as indicated by the "official story".

Consequently, Dr. Harris is factually incorrect when he tries to claim that there were no leaks concerning 9/11. Rather, there were all kinds of leaks, but those leaks also were accompanied by an array of efforts on the part of the government and the mainstream media to contain and suppress the foregoing sorts of information.

Furthermore, even if one were to concede Dr. Harris's point that there were no leaks concerning the events of 9/11, nonetheless, if – as Dr. Harris states in the extended statement that was quoted at the beginning of this section of the present chapter – conspiracy thinking claims that psychopathic individuals collaborated in the killing of people in Manhattan on 9/11, then, none of those psychopathic will have the requisite guilty conscience that is likely to lead them to make the sort of public confessions on 60 Minutes that would constitute the kind of leak that Dr. Harris seems to have in mind. Thus, even if it had been the case that there were no leaks concerning the events of 9/11

– which is factually untrue – if psychopaths really were in charge of the 9/11 operations, then, one would have no reason to expect that any leaks would be forthcoming since, by definition, psychopaths are individuals who do things without remorse for the harm they cause to others, and therefore, they do not experience guilty consciences in relation to the things they do or don't do.

One also should keep in mind some rather sobering revelations that appear in research concerning psychopaths (such as: *Without Conscience: The Disturbing World of The Psychopaths Among Us* by Robert D. Hare; *Snakes In Suits* by Paul Babiak and Robert Hare; *The Sociopath Next Door* by Martha Stout, and *The Psychopath* by James Blair, Derek Mitchell, and Karina Blair). For instance, a conservative estimate of the number of psychopaths that live among us is between 10 and 13,000,000 million individuals, and those individuals occupy all strata of society including: Government, the military, science, law enforcement, the media, the judiciary, banking, education, and the corporate world.

The power structure is infested with such individuals. If some aspect of that power structure were interested in perpetrating a crime like 9/11, it would have little trouble recruiting people from within its own ranks that possessed the right sort of psychopathic tendencies to be able to plan, implement, and cover-up something like 9/11, and there are millions of other individuals who, if necessary, could be psychologically manipulated into becoming ideological psychopaths who could play the role of "useful idiots" on behalf of such psychopathic "leadership" (Ideological psychopaths are individuals who are so entangled in, and committed to, their system of beliefs that they are willing to adopt psychopathic-like traits – such as a relative absence of compassion and conscience – in order to impose their beliefs on other human beings).

In his earlier, extended statement, Dr. Harris alludes to the ideas of some individuals who argue that the motivation for 9/11 was to create a pretext that would be able to justify going to war in Iraq in order to afford the United States an opportunity to take control of Iraq's oil. Dr. Harris questions the logic underlying such thinking by citing the fact that none of the hijackers came from Iraq and, therefore, if the motivation for 9/11 had been to provide justification for attacking Iraq, then, surely, a better scenario could have been arranged than getting non-Iraqis to hijack airplanes and crash them into various targets in the United States

Dr. Harris should be less arbitrary and selective (in a self-serving manner) with respect to the possible motivations concerning the perpetration of 9/11 that he considers. However, by framing the issue in the way he has – namely, that some people believe that 9/11 was used as a pretext for invading Iraq – he is able to ignore a

litany of other possibilities concerning the kinds of
motivations that might have been behind 9/11.

For example, on – and/or prior to -- 9/11,
hundreds of billions of dollars worth of gold were
removed from the vaults of the Bank of Nova Scotia
beneath Building 4 of the World Trade Center. In
addition, billions of dollars worth of insurance
fraud, bond market manipulations involving Brady
bonds, and problematic stock market transactions
(in relation to American and United Airlines, as
well as in relation to a variety of companies that
were located in the Twin Towers of the World
Trade Center) also were committed in conjunction
with 9/11.

Moreover, the Office of Naval Investigation and
the Army Audit Office had been given the task of
investigating the 2.1 trillion dollars that were
reported as having gone MIA by Donald Rumsfeld
the day before 9/11. The offices where the two
foregoing investigatory units were located
happened to be among the ones that were
destroyed at the Pentagon on 9/11.

Furthermore, Building 7 of the World Trade
Center contained considerable evidence concerning
the multi-million dollar scams of, among others,
Enron, World Com, and Global Crossing. All of that
evidence was destroyed on September 11, 2001.

9/11 was also used as a pretext for rushing to
pass The Patriot Act that already had been written
prior to 9/11 and for which its proponents were
merely awaiting the right opportunity to be able to

introduce it into Congress. Moreover, 9/11 served as the motivating pretext for the creation of Homeland Security, which became a cash cow worth billions of dollars as well as a means of gaining increased control over the citizens of America.

Furthermore, the first war to be declared after 9/11 was not in Iraq, but in Afghanistan, and that war was tied directly to 9/11 – despite a lack of proof – as a result of charging the Taliban with harboring the person who was considered by the U.S. government to be the master-mind of 9/11 – namely, 'Usama bin Laden – again, despite the official admission of the FBI that there was no evidence tying bin Laden to 9/11. Moreover, notwithstanding that to which Dr, Harris alludes in relation to his previously given extended statement, there would have been no reason to attack Saudi Arabia because although many of the alleged 19 hijackers supposedly were from Saudi Arabia, nevertheless, those individuals were characterized as a bunch of disaffected individuals who had broken ranks with the Saudi government because the latter had permitted infidels to set up bases on holy land during the first Gulf War, and, therefore, presumably, Saudi Arabia was not responsible for what those disaffected individuals did and, as a result, could not be considered to be a state sponsor of terrorism.

In addition, contrary to what Dr. Harris claims, Cheney, Bush, and others did come up with a variety of other pretexts in addition to September 11th, for going to war with Iraq. Aside from the fact that Cheney insisted that there had been contact between al-Qaeda and Saddam Hussein that took place in Czechoslovakia, Hungary, Romania or some such place, Bush, Powell, and Blair invented the idea that there were weapons of mass destruction in Iraq despite the fact that the UN indicated that there were no weapons of mass destruction remaining in Iraq (Hans Blix was head of the United Nations Monitoring, Verification, and Inspection Commission from January 2000 to June 2003 and American Scott Ritter, Jr. was a weapons inspector for the United Nations from 1991 to 1998, and both of the foregoing individuals stated prior to the 2003 invasion of Iraq that, up to that point in time, no significant cache of weapons of mass destruction were being stockpiled in Iraq).

Finally, in his previous quoted extended statement, Dr. Harris takes a fictitious example – i.e., the next iPhone being left at a bar before it is released – and tries to claim (without evidence) that such a contrafactual example is relevant to what took place in relation to 9/11 by creating the impression that if 9/11 had been the result of the actions of individuals other than bin-Laden and 19 Arab hijackers, then there would have been leaks of one kind or another ... but, according to Dr. Harris, no such leaks have occurred. The fact of the matter is that quite independently of the already mentioned instances of government officials such as Sibel Edmonds, Robert Wright, Jr., Colonel

70

Anthony Schaefer, Coleen Rowley, Barry Jennings, David Schippers and many others who tried to get their testimony included in the public record concerning 9/11, there also <u>were</u> other leaks concerning 9/11. For example, one might consider the notice released prior to the events of 9/11 by Odigo (an Israeli instant messaging service) warning roughly 4,000 people to stay away from the World Trade Center on 9/11, or, perhaps more importantly, there is the sworn testimony of April Gallop – who was at Ground Zero in the Pentagon at the time that explosions occurred – which stipulated that she saw no evidence indicating that a plane had hit the Pentagon on 9/11 and also testified that several people who did not identify themselves came to the hospital where she and her baby were being treated for injuries due to events taking place on 9/11, and those individuals tried to intimidate her into silence with respect to what she had seen and experienced at the Pentagon on 9/11.

When it comes to 9/11, clearly, Sam Harris seems to know almost nothing – if not nothing – about the events of that day. The thinking that is problematic concerning 9/11 is entirely his, and Dr. Harris is the source for some of the very fake news phenomenon that he purports to be critically opposed to in his foregoing comments.

Nonetheless, Sam Harris is quite correct. When one connects the issue of fake news with Dr. Harris's sort of conspiracy thinking (his thinking is conspiratorial not only in relation to what the critics of 9/11 are all about, but, as well, his belief that al-Qaeda is responsible for 9/11 is also conspiratorial), then, the results are "hugely consequential" because his brand of fake news might, very well, have helped facilitate the deaths of millions of Muslims and other individuals in the Middle East, as well as might have helped enable the displacement, abuse, mutilation, and destruction of millions of Iraqi and Afghani lives by the United States government and others.

The following excerpts are from another podcast in which Sam Harris participated that pertains to the issues of 9/11. I'll begin with an extended quote from this second podcast that features some of the views of Sam Harris concerning 9/11, followed by some critical reflection on what he says, and, then, move on to address other excerpts from that same, second podcast.

"If you ask someone who really believes in the 9/11 truth conspiracy theory, right, that Bush brought down the World Trade Center, and you ask them to have a conversation about it, and they give you all the rigmarole about the melting point of steel and building 7 and people rigged the buildings to explode, and you ask them how they got all that thermite into the buildings, and they did it in the dead of night, and how many conspirators were involved, and there's an endless energy to talk about these things, and in that case these really are propositional claims about what happened when no one was looking, and I think the people who believe this stuff really do believe it, and this is very much analogous to what happens in religions ... this is analogous to a Christian saying: "No, No, you don't understand. I really think that Jesus was resurrected. I think he was nailed up on the cross, he was a human being. The tomb was empty, and he ascended ... and what do you think ascension is? Well, I think it's actually going up against gravity physically, and when the rapture happens, I'm going to be pulled up there, and if you're in a 747 at that moment, you're going to see me up in the stratosphere. Whether they are that explicit, if you get people talking, they believe something concrete ... they're not metaphorical moves."

Why is Dr. Harris's litmus-test for 9/11 a matter of whether, or not, someone believes that Bush is responsible for what went on that day? Why doesn't Dr. Harris – or the conversation he claims to want to have with someone who engages 9/11 in a way that is different from him – start with the fact that the official story does not hold together and, therefore, whatever happened on that day is other than what the official story – or Dr. Harris -- is trying to suggest?

How does one have a conversation with someone – such as Dr. Harris -- who refers to the issue of facts as "rigmarole"? The use of that term seems to provide evidence that Dr. Harris is a person who already has made up his mind about the issue of 9/11, and, as a result, uses a pejorative term to sum up what he believes concerning matters that appear to be closed for him as far as further inquiry of a sincere, objective nature is concerned.

In a real conversation – that is, a dialogue – two, or more, individuals mutually explore possibilities in order to try to discover the nature of truth involving some matter, but all Dr. Harris seems to want to do is to ask questions in an incorrect order and in an obstructionist manner. For instance, instead of asking – as Dr. Harris does -- how people got thermite into the Trade Towers, (and thermite is a mixture of powdered iron oxide and aluminum capable of generating very high temperatures when ignited), why not ask why traces of military grade nano-thermite have been found in dust samples from Ground Zero (and nano-thermite consists of a metal and metal oxide whose particles are combined in powders that are 100 nanometers in size), or why not ask Dr. Harris to defend the official story concerning the events of 9/11?

Instead, Dr. Harris asks questions for which he knows there are logistical problems and for which there is, at best, only marginal and rather speculative "evidence." Doing things in this manner offers him a way to frame the conversation in a way that serves his interests ... in other words, the foregoing approach gives expression to an underlying strategy in which certain kinds of questions are asked or raised in order to obscure, or detract attention away from, more pertinent and fundamental kinds of questions.

For instance, the theory that Bush brought down the World Trade Center might be a theory that is advanced by some individuals, but such an idea doesn't necessarily have anything to do with the fact that three World Trade Buildings came down at near free fall speed on 9/11 and that this latter set of facts is completely inconsistent with the "official" explanation that planes and fires caused three buildings at the World Trade Center to collapse. In other words, one should separate the issue of who is responsible for 9/11 from the issue of the physical evidence that exists in conjunction with the events at the World Trade Center, the Pentagon, and Shanksville, Pennsylvania.

Before trying to decide who perpetrated the events of 9/11, perhaps, the first order of business should be to determine the nature of the events that transpired on that day. For example, before claiming that 19 Arabs were the ones who attacked America on 9/11, maybe one should try to determine what the evidence is concerning whether, or not, 19 Arabs actually hijacked four planes, or whether, or not, those individuals could have flown commercial jets in the way indicated by the "official story", or whether, or not, cell phones could have been used to make calls from airplanes at heights above 1,500 feet, or whether, or not, planes and/or fires would have been able to cause three steel-framed buildings to collapse in the way indicated by the official story, or whether, or not, a plane hit the Pentagon, or whether, or not, a plane actually crashed in Shanksville, Pennsylvania.

In the previously quoted, extended excerpt from one of his podcasts, Dr. Harris notes that the people who harbor all kinds of beliefs concerning the events of 9/11 are making propositional claims about what happened when no one was looking. Furthermore, Dr. Harris claims that this is very similar to what takes place in conjunction with religious claims when people give expression to various beliefs about, for instance, the crucifixion and resurrection of Jesus or what happens during the phenomenon of "rapture" despite the fact that those individuals have no access to hard evidence concerning those sorts of matters.

While it might be true that some people make statements about 9/11 that are divorced from, or contradicted by, actual facts concerning the events of that day, nonetheless -- and notwithstanding Dr. Harris's propositional claims to the contrary -- the issues of 9/11 are not at all like the religious issues that Dr. Harris mentions. There is a considerable amount of factual evidence that exists in relation to the events of 9/11 that are, for the most part, absent from an array of religious issues.

For instance, commercial jets could not have flown at the speeds indicated by the official story concerning 9/11. Such speeds exceeded – by hundreds of miles per hour -- the VMO, or the maximum permitted operating speeds for such aircrafts and would have led to substantial structural damage to aircraft flying at those speeds. Or, contrary to the claims of NIST, Underwriters Laboratories empirically demonstrated that the floor assembly units for the Twin Tower buildings would not have failed in the way in which NIST claimed they did on 9/11, and, therefore, the failure of those assemblies could not have been a cause of the progressive collapse of the two towers as stated by NIST with respect to the events of 9/11.

Kevin Ryan, a chemist, was fired from his job at Underwriters Laboratories for disclosing the foregoing information. This is, yet, another fact that discredits the view of Dr. Harris that there were no leaks that occurred in conjunction with the events of 9/11.

Furthermore, independently of the logistical problems raised by Dr. Harris concerning how people (or how many people were required to) get thermite into the Twin Towers, or when this was done, and quite independently of whether, at this point, those questions can be determinately answered, one is confronted with the fact that Mark Basile, a chemical engineer, along with a number of other scientists (e.g., Steven Jones, a physicist, Kevin Ryan, a chemist, and Niels Harrit, a chemist), have found evidence that military grade nano-thermite was present in different dust samples that were taken from Ground Zero. This fact needs to be explained because there is no good reason for nano-thermite to be present in those dust samples ... in other words, military grade nano-thermite is not something that will naturally form in dust without a great deal of highly technical assistance.

In addition, quite apart from Dr. Harris's dismissal of such allegedly rigmarole issues as the melting point of steel, many scientifically and technically oriented observers have commented that fires and heat cannot account for the total pulverization of nearly a million tons of: Steel beams, concrete, acres of marble surfacing, numerous multi-ton electrical transformers, as well as office furniture that took place at the World Trade Towers on 9/11. The phenomenon of progressive collapse -- which is put forth by NIST as the reason why three steel-framed structures collapsed on 9/11 -- is not capable of generating the level of force that could cause the foregoing kind of destruction.

Progressive collapses are a function of the force of gravity. Yet, whatever caused the pulverization of more than one million tons of materials on 9/11 at the World Trade Center involved a force or forces that is, or are, far in excess of what gravity can deliver through a progressive collapse.

Another empirical fact that is present with respect to 9/11 is that air-phones could not have been used to make phone calls, as claimed in the official story, on some of the planes supposedly hijacked on 9/11 – namely, American Airlines Flights 11 and 77. Air phones had been deactivated on all American Airline flights as of January 31, 2001, nearly nine months prior to 9/11.

Consequently, Barbara Olson – who, supposedly, was a passenger on Flight 77 -- could not have used an air-phone on 9/11 to call her husband, Ted Olson, the Solicitor General for the United States. As noted above, all such phones had been deactivated by American Airlines and, therefore, were not available on Flight 77.

Furthermore, contrary to the claims of the official story, Barbara Olson could not have used a cell phone to make a collect call to her husband. This is because not only do cell phones not operate in such a fashion, but, as well, because cell phones in 2001 were not capable of working in planes flying at altitude which is when the calls from Barbara Olson to Ted Olson supposedly were made.

Finally – although many other facts could be cited here – according to the official story, no plane parts were found at the alleged 9/11 crash sites in New York City, Virginia (the Pentagon), or Shanksville, Pennsylvania. Yet, 80,000 pieces of the Columbia shuttle were retrieved despite the fact that the shuttle was traveling at 17,000 miles per hour when it disintegrated while the hijacked planes of 9/11 were only flying at 4-500 miles an hour when they supposedly disintegrated.

Airplanes don't disintegrate when they impact the ground or a building. And, yet, according to the official story concerning 9/11, we are being asked to believe – despite a total lack of any evidence or proof – that for the first time in aviation history, four commercial jets all disintegrated on impact on the same day and left nothing behind except a couple of paper passports (one on the streets of New York and the other in a field in Shanksville) that, quite by chance, happened to belong to several of the alleged hijackers.

In short, Dr. Harris contends that claims made in relation to 9/11 are like claims made in a religious context because – according to Dr. Harris – in both instances propositional statements are being made about events that are devoid of the sort of facts that are needed to support the propositional statements that are being made. Although there could be specific instances in which the foregoing contention might be substantiated with respect to the claims that some individuals make in conjunction with 9/11, nonetheless, as a general statement concerning 9/11, his contention is ludicrous because – as has been noted throughout this chapter -- there are many facts that can be consulted in relation to 9/11 that one cannot access in various religious issues.

Following up on the previously quoted extended excerpt from a second podcast concerning 9/11, Sam Harris goes on to say:

"There's no question that people sometimes conspire, right, so I already have a room in this unexplored mansion ... it's completely rational for me to open that door. I'm not forsaking any principle of rationality to say: This might be among the conspiracies that I haven't heard about. It only becomes irrational – like in the case of 9/11 truth – for me when I see that (1) the incentives are not aligned the way they should be; (2) the number of conspirators are so vast as to make any effective secrecy implausible; (3) the kind of reasoning that I notice people doing in order to defend the anomalies there become ... it's so obviously post hoc and based on confirmation bias, and a host of cognitive errors that the defenses are not plausible, but if you change all of that, and you give me an allegation, about an egregious conspiracy that is more well-behaved ... where you don't require 5,000 conspirators, and it is not all pieced together after the fact, and the incentives make some sense, then I have a category for that which is, yes, sometimes there really are mustache-twirling conspirators who have access to information that we don't have and they operate in darkness, and we find out 30 years later, and, yes, it's true that for me to spend any time entertaining that in a condition where it is not yet plausible or not popular ... yeah, that is kind of a faith-based use of my time ... I'm saying, well, is this worth doing ... am I going to look crazy to my peers?"

In the foregoing comments, Dr. Harris contends that -- depending on circumstances – although the idea of conspiracy is not necessarily irrational, nevertheless, he considers 9/11 claims to be irrational. He proceeds to cite three rules of reasoning [involving (1) proper alignment of incentives, (2) the number of conspirators, and (3) the kind of reasoning employed) that, supposedly, help lead him to the conclusion that 9/11 claims are irrational in nature.

Why should one accept Dr. Harris's foregoing conditions of rationality, or why should one accept his way of applying those conditions to the issue of 9/11? There is nothing in the contents of that podcast from which the foregoing excerpt is drawn that provides anything of a persuasive nature that might induce one to adopt his proposed rules for reasoning about 9/11.

He only addresses – in a very oblique manner – a few possibilities in his remarks, and, then, appears to conclude that because some ideas concerning 9/11 might be irrational, then, all ideas concerning 9/11 must be irrational. In other words, Dr. Harris seems to be classifying all 9/11 ideas that differ from the prevailing story (the "official" view) as being irrational.

However, he fails to demonstrate that his position is tenable. Among other things, in this regard, Dr. Harris doesn't tackle any central or fundamental issue concerning 9/11 ... not the least of which is that there is absolutely nothing about the prevailing/official view, story or theory concerning 9/11 that is tenable, and, therefore, by necessity, one is forced to search for some other way to account for the events of 9/11.

One also might point out that in conjunction with his aforementioned first rule of reasoning concerning 9/11 Dr. Harris doesn't specify what the nature of the incentives are that should be aligned in a certain way, nor does he specify the nature of the criteria that are to be used in determining what constitutes a proper alignment of incentives, nor does he justify the use of those unspecified criteria for establishing a proper alignment of incentives. In short, Dr. Harris first rule or principle of reasoning concerning 9/11 is devoid of specific content or any sort of rationale for why it should be used to identify what is rational when it comes to the issue of 9/11.

As far as the second rule or principle of reasoning that is employed by Dr. Harris to make judgments about the rationality of any given perspective concerning 9/11 – namely, the matter of how many conspirators are required to pull off 9/11 – one wonders how many conspirators are required to make something implausible, and what is the basis for making such a claim? The second rule or principle of reasoning cited by Dr. Harris seems both arbitrary and subjective.

What he considers implausible might not actually be so. Among other things, he has no idea – or, at least, his foregoing comments contain no evidence in this respect -- about what secrets might have been kept successfully by the government or about how many people might have been involved in keeping those secrets.

84

After all, there were a reported 125,000 people involved in the Manhattan Project during its peak period of hiring (and this does not take into account the total, cumulative number of people who were hired, for one reason or another, for just short periods of time at some point during the project). Yet, nonetheless, that secret appeared to be kept fairly well while it was taking place.

At a subsequent juncture in his foregoing comments, Dr. Harris mentions that 5,000 people constitute a conspiracy that is not well-behaved. This seems to be a rather arbitrary figure (and claim) and, therefore, stands in need of being justified ... something that Dr. Harris does not do.

In addition, there could be a lot fewer people needed to keep a significant secret hidden than Dr. Harris appears to suppose is necessary. For example, a great deal of information might be capable of being controlled by a few individuals and, then, altered as necessary in order to provide different people with various cover stories concerning what is taking place, and, as a result, many individuals whose understanding of what is transpiring might be manipulated by the kind of information they are being fed and, therefore, they could be participating in a set of events such as 9/11 without understanding the actual significance of their participation or how that participation serves a secret purpose or project that might be orchestrated through the control of information concerning those events.

During his foregoing extended comments, Dr. Harris also alludes to individuals who supposedly reason about 9/11 in, allegedly, an ad hoc fashion or individuals who base their understanding on confirmation bias, or individuals who commit other kinds of cognitive errors. However, he provides no specific examples of what he means.

Therefore, one has no way of knowing whether what he claims he has noticed in conjunction with such 9/11 thinking is really the case or whether what he saying in this regard merely gives expression to his own set of cognitive errors. In fact, to proceed in the vague, non-specific way that he does in the context of 9/11 is to commit a cognitive error, because, without specificity, what he says is devoid of substantive value.

Dr. Harris also advances the idea in his foregoing, extended comments about the allegedly problematic way in which conspiracy thinkers are "defending" various views concerning 9/11 anomalies. However, Dr. Harris doesn't specify what sorts of anomalies he has in mind at this point, nor does he stipulate what the nature of the defense is concerning those anomalies or why such defenses are problematic.

Before trying to analyze whether, or not, certain ways of defending various anomalies are viable, one, first, should become clear about the nature of the anomalies one is talking about in order to determine whether, or not, some ways of defending a perspective concerning various anomalies might be better than others. For instance, one might critically reflect on the manner in which the prevailing/official view, story or theory seeks to explain away (or dismiss) various anomalies -- such as the issue of bombs going off at the World Trade Center or the free-fall speed exhibited during the demise of the three building at that complex, or, the alleged crash of planes at the Trade Towers – by, for the most part, largely ignoring all manner of evidence concerning the foregoing matters that is inconsistent with the story the government and the mainstream media wish to promulgate.

At a certain point in the previously quoted extended comment, Dr, Harris talks, in a pejorative fashion, about piecing things together after the fact. Just what does he mean?

Most understanding and knowledge is pieced together after the fact. This is a common process in both science and everyday life in which we try to make sense of the data or information that is available to us but tend to do so after the fact, rather, than prior to the fact. Is Dr. Harris suggesting that people should generate their understanding before the fact of events?

At a certain point in his extended comments, Dr. Harris speaks about waiting until an idea is plausible or popular before deciding whether, or not, to invest time in such an issue. He also notes, in passing, that he does not wish to look crazy in the eyes of his peers.

The truth is not necessarily about people's conception of what is, or is not, plausible nor is it a matter of popularity. Furthermore, searching for the truth should not be a function of one's concern with what others think about what one is doing because this merely means that one is permitting other people to set the agenda for the pursuit of truth, and, consequently, one becomes susceptible to a process of self-censorship in which one shies away from tackling certain issues because of the opinions that other individuals have concerning those matters.

Of course, when investigating any given issue, one should take into consideration what other people – especially one's peers – believe. Nonetheless, one needs to independently reflect on those beliefs in order to determine whether, or not, the beliefs of one's peers should be taken seriously and considered to be reliable.

In many cases one only can determine the "worth" of doing something after the fact of having done it. This is one of the reasons why people conduct experiments or why they explore different aspects of existence in order to find out what worth, if any, is entailed by such activities ... and, often times, discovering problems can have as much worth – and, sometimes has more worth – than discovering certain kinds of truths.

In his foregoing, extended comments, despite citing three rules or principles of reasoning concerning 9/11, Dr. Harris fails to specify what it is about the issue of 9/11 that is irrational, or implausible, or not worth the effort to try to discover what the truth concerning 9/11 actually is. Dr. Harris refers to alternative approaches to 9/11 as being inherently implausible, and, yet, rather than examine, in concrete terms, the actual evidence concerning such matters, he restricts himself to talking only in vague generalities about allegedly problematic, conspiratorial approaches to 9/11, and, lo and behold, he finds that alternative ideas about 9/11 are, ipso facto, implausible ... as computer programmers might say: Garbage in and, therefore, garbage out.

In addition to two podcasts (discussed above) that contain material on Dr. Harris's ideas about 9/11, Sam Harris also was a guest on 'The Joe Rogan Experience" where he discussed such issues. "The Joe Rogan Experience is an Internet program that explores – through interviews and commentary -- a variety of issues.

During the foregoing program, Dr. Harris states:

"The problem with any conspiracy of that sort, and especially a bigger one, like 9/11 truth stuff conspiracy is that it just takes so much perfect collaboration to bring it off, and we know that people are so bad at that ... we know that interests don't align so perfectly ... we know that there's always somebody who just wants to sell their story to a tabloid, or feels guilty about the part they played ... or, they're getting divorced and they just can't stop talking ... and Bill Clinton couldn't keep a semen-stained dress off of the news. You know that's like the simplest thing. He is like the President of the United States with a terrified intern, and this is going to wreck his presidency, and he still couldn't keep the dress a secret."

To begin with, Dr. Harris offers no evidence or proof in the foregoing statement (or later in the program) demonstrating that conspiracies require "perfect collaboration" in order for them to be perpetrated. Furthermore, the term: "perfect collaboration" frames his perspective gives expression to an arbitrary standard that he claims is necessary for a conspiracy to be perpetrated, and, consequently, that standard is something that he needs to justify ... which he does not do during the aforementioned program..

In addition, the foregoing excerpt from his interview with Joe Rogan seems to provide fairly clear evidence that Dr. Harris wishes to use many, if not all, of his comments concerning 9/11 by playing them off against various 'conspiracy theories'. Yet, not all things 9/11 are necessarily about conspiracies.

Unfortunately, however, Dr. Harris doesn't appear to want to talk about the actual issues, problems and evidence that pertain to 9/11. Indeed, during the course of nearly 70 minutes of recorded material (involving two podcasts and the Joe Rogan interview), Sam Harris fails to offer even one fact about the actual events of 9/11 ... everything he says in the aforementioned recorded material is based on generalized, unsupported statements concerning purported conspiracy theories.

Furthermore, Dr. Harris not only limits his remarks concerning 9/11 to the topic of conspiracy theory, but he also seems to want to talk only about certain kinds of conspiracies ... ones that don't make sense or that involve problems of one kind or another. Apparently, he is trying to distance himself (and everyone else) from the real issues of 9/11, and if this is not what he is trying to accomplish, then, nevertheless, this is the inevitable result of the manner in which he seems to approach issues involving 9/11.

Dr. Harris continuously places the cart before the horse when it comes to 9/11. For example, rather than taking the time to sift through the evidence concerning the prevailing or official view/story and its attendant problems, he chooses

to address the issue of collaboration and how it
needs to be so perfect in order to be pulled off.

Who is responsible for 9/11 – irrespective of
whether, or not, the perpetration of such a crime is
done with perfect collaboration -- is not the first
order of business in any investigation of 9/11. To
properly initiate an investigation into 9/11, one
needs to try to establish what happened on that
day.

Once the foregoing has been accomplished,
then, one could proceed to critically entertain
different theories about possible responsibility. In
other words, once a person has established some
basic facts, then, an individual might be in a
position to determine whether, or not, any of those
kinds of theories are defensible, or indefensible,
ways to account for the facts that have been
established.

According to Dr. Harris's earlier quoted
statement on the Joe Rogan program, "we"
allegedly know all kinds of things about
conspiracies. For example, supposedly, we know
that people are bad at keeping conspiracies secret
and, supposedly, we know "there's always
somebody who wants to sell their story to a
tabloid", and so on.

Apparently, we know all kinds of things that
aren't necessarily so. For instance, we might know
that some people are bad at keeping secrets, but we
have no way of knowing if everybody is bad at
doing so.

Conceivably, there are people who are really good at keeping secrets and/or at collaborating with one another to maintain secrecy. Presumably, such people would be very hard to identify and, therefore, might stand a good chance of being able to elude detection.

Moreover, contrary to the foregoing contention of Dr. Harris, we don't necessarily know that there always will be somebody who wants to talk about a conspiracy or that there always will be someone who has a guilty conscience concerning things in which they were involved. To be sure, we might know there are <u>some</u> people who are willing to talk or who have a guilty conscience because we have come across such cases in our own lives or through the news or on television or in books.

Nevertheless, we are not necessarily likely to know about cases in which the people involved with a given event were unwilling to talk about what went on, or unwilling to sell their story, or did not have a guilty conscience concerning such matters. By purporting that we know all the things he claims we know with respect to the issue of conspiracies, Dr. Harris is putting forth a theory that requires something more than his assertions about such matters.

In addition, as was the case with respect to one of the podcasts involving Dr. Harris was discussed previously in this chapter, he, once again, refers to the Bill Clinton example concerning a semen-stained dress, and Dr. Harris appears to believe that just one example – the one he keeps repeating – is capable of proving his point about the difficulty involved with suppressing evidence. However, all his example demonstrates is that there are some things that have not been kept a secret.

The Bill Clinton case is part of an inductive argument. Dr. Harris is trying to argue from the particulars of the Bill Clinton issue to conspiracy theories in general by arguing that as Bill Clinton goes, so go all attempts to keep things secret, but he needs something more than one anecdotal case to give credence to the point he is trying to make.

In other words, the form of Dr. Harris's argument at this point is that conspiracies are highly unlikely to be successful because all one has to do verify such a contention is to look at the Bill Clinton case involving Monika Lewinsky and the semen-stained dress. Yet, Dr. Harris does not offer any relevant evidence concerning how many conspiracies are successful and remain hidden as measured against how many conspiracies are not successful or do not remain hidden … a statistic that might serve to support his view that the Bill Clinton case is fairly typical of what happens when people try to keep things secret or quiet.

Consequently, what Bill Clinton could, or could not, do with respect to the suppression of evidence doesn't necessarily have anything to do with the issues of 9/11. One needs to ask, among other things, whether, or not, the official theory concerning 9/11 is tenable, and, if it is not – which I do not believe it is, and this is a belief rooted in considerable evidence (some of which has been indicated previously in this chapter and much more of which can be found in several books on the subject that I have written) -- then, one must go in search of some alternative account to explain the events of 9/11.

Plausibility concerning the nature of the events that transpired on 9/11 must come from the evidence entailed by 9/11. Plausibility will not be found – as Dr. Harris seems wont to do -- through the processing of irrelevant information – such as the activities of Bill Clinton in the Oval Office – or by speculating, in a general manner, about conspiracies of one kind or another.

To reiterate a point made earlier, first, one must ask if the prevailing/official view is capable of being defended, and irrespective – at this point – of how such a set of events might have been pulled off or how unlikely such a process might have been, if the "official" view, theory, or story is not tenable, then one is left with the realization that although somebody did pull something off on 9/11 because the evidence supports such a claim, but, nonetheless, the somebody who did pull something off did not necessarily include the 19 hijackers from Saudi Arabia and a few other Middle Eastern countries who were identified by the FBI as having perpetrated 9/11 because according to the BBC and various other sources, at least ten of those individuals are still alive, and none of the names of any of the alleged hijackers appeared on the passenger manifest lists for Flights 11, 175, 77, or 93.

Dr. Harris continues on in the Joe Rogan interview with the following comments:

"There's an adage on this subject – never ascribe to conspiracy what can be explained by incompetence, or something like that, and it's just so obvious the incompetence factor in many of these situations is so high and so obvious … and with September 11th, it's just a crushing variable … we were just not … we're not prepared to deal with that kind of problem, and anyone who thinks this was a conspiracy thinks that at least hundreds, probably thousands of people woke up one day – perfectly normal people … people in the FAA, people in the military, people in government … woke up perfect psychopaths willing with a clear conscience to murder 3,000 of their innocent neighbors and not … this wasn't Tuskegee …this wasn't the poor and disenfranchised of a race that you're not so fond of … these are some of the most powerful people in our society just blown up one day and all of this was perfectly attuned to leave the person at the top of the conspiracy -- presumably George Bush -- sitting reading *My Pet Goat* when the whole thing kicked off I mean it's just … it's ridiculous … it's like … and, then, as a pretext to go into Iraq … first of all, it would have been so much easier to think of a pretext to go into Iraq, but why make it look like we got bombed or attacked by Saudis, and Yemenis and Egyptians which, in fact, is what it looks like?

... If your thinking about the sort of false flag operation thesis ... that we wanted to go into Iraq and steal their oil ... but, then, we're perfectly evil and perfectly Machiavellian and could bring this whole thing off without any leaks to this day... ten years hence, no one has come forward and said this is the part I played in it, and I feel terrible about it, and, yet, we botched it in these huge ways where we had to go to Afghanistan, before Iraq, and we really didn't want to go to Afghanistan ... no one suggests we actually wanted to actually wanted to be running around Tora Bora fighting the Taliban."

Can incompetence – as Dr. Harris claims -- really explain 9/11? For example, can one attribute the fact that three Trade Towers fell that day at roughly freefall speeds into their own footprint as being due to incompetence? Was the fact that most of the Twin Towers and Building 7 had been transformed into dust on 9/11 – something that could not be accomplished by airplane crashes, fires, and collapses – due to incompetence? Was the fact that none of the phone calls from the allegedly hijacked airplanes that day – most of which were cellular in nature – could not possibly have been made from those planes when they were in the air due to incompetence? Was the fact that there was no airplane wreckage found at the Pentagon due to incompetence? Was the fact that at least ten of the alleged hijackers – including (according to his parents) Mohammed Atta -- were still alive after 9/11 due to incompetence? Was the fact that professional commercial and military pilots have indicated that they could not have hit those buildings that day in the manner indicated in the official story due to incompetence? Is the fact that no steel-structured building prior to, or since 9/11, ever collapsed due to fires despite having burned for up to 20 times as long as the Trade Towers due to incompetence? Is the fact that none of the pilots or flight attendants in the four, allegedly hijacked airplanes followed FAA protocol that day due to incompetence? Is the fact that William Rodriguez and others heard and experienced bombs going off in the Twin Towers <u>before</u> planes supposedly struck those buildings due to incompetence? Is the fact that none of the alleged hijackers ever flew anything more than a single-engine airplane and were considered to be poor or terrible pilots by their instructors, and, yet, somehow on 9/11 were able to fly commercial jets better than pilots with many years experience were able to do, due to incompetence? Is the fact that for months after 9/11 temperatures in excess of 1,000 degrees Fahrenheit were recorded at Ground Zero despite the fact there was no identifiable source of fuel to sustain such temperatures for that length of time due to incompetence? Does the fact that April Gallop – who was at the Pentagon when things blew up on 9/11 – was willing to testify in a sworn statement that there were no plane wreckage, engines, luggage, bodies or fires in the space where the incident happened due to incompetence? Was the fact that 12 witnesses – including members of the Pentagon police – have given public statements that the plane that approached the Pentagon on 9/11 flew on the North side of the Citgo gas station about a mile from the Pentagon and not on the South side of that station as required by the Official story due to incompetence?

In addition, Dr. Harris appears to be proposing something quite remarkable in his previous comments when he appears to suggest that the events of September 11th are entirely explicable as a function of incompetence. More specifically, according to Dr. Harris, 20 Arabs (consisting of 19 alleged hijackers and a guy in a cave in Afghanistan) were able to collaborate with sufficient competence to pull off 9/11, but, for whatever reason, such collaborative competence seems to be beyond the ability of Americans because, as Dr. Harris confidently states, everybody "knows" how bad at conspiracies and keeping secrets that people in government are.

Furthermore, in the previous extended statement that has been quoted, Dr. Harris advances a theory – based on a fictitious conspiracy scenario -- concerning the alleged cognitive states of the people who might have committed 9/11. More specifically, according to Dr. Harris, first, those who were responsible for 9/11 were perfectly normal, and, then, they became psychopaths.

However, the argument is entirely constructed from suppositions that are not tied to any actual analysis of the people who were responsible for 9/11 ... whoever they might be. He has no idea – and, certainly, no evidence to substantiate such an idea -- whether, or not, the perpetrators were normal individuals, or whether there was some transformation in them through which they became psychopaths ... this is all contra-factual thinking ... on the part of both Dr. Harris as well as on the part of any conspiracy theory that might be making such claims.

At this point in the previously quoted excerpt from the Joe Rogan Experience interview, Dr. Harris launches into a soliloquy against those who believe that the attacks of 9/11 were a pretext for invading Iraq despite the fact that the alleged hijackers were, supposedly, from Saudi Arabia, Yemen, and Egypt. As he does so, he attempts to downplay the fact that the first war to be declared after 9/11 involved Afghanistan by trying to claim that no one wanted to go into Afghanistan. However, if this is the case, then, why did the United States reject, out of hand, the Taliban offer to be willing to hand over 'Usama bin Laden on the presentation of proof by the United States that he was, indeed, responsible for 9/11?

NATO's rules of engagement with respect to Afghanistan also required the foregoing sort of proof. However, just as the United States government never provided that proof to the Taliban government, the American government also never produced such proof for NATO, and, therefore, NATO's participation in the Afghan war constitutes a violation of that alliance's charter.

Furthermore, if, as Dr. Harris claims, the United States government was not interested in going into Afghanistan, then, why did the American government indicate that its reason for war with Afghanistan had to do with the fact that the Taliban had been giving safe harbor to 'Usama bin Laden and other members of al-Qaeda, and since those individuals were responsible for 9/11, then, Afghan must be taught a lesson concerning its support of such terrorists and criminals? This reason for war was given despite the fact – previously noted -- that the FBI indicated on its web site that bin Laden was not wanted for 9/11, and, as well, Robert Mueller – the, then, Director of the FBI -- also indicated, when asked, that the FBI had no evidence that tied bin Laden to the events of 9/11?

To try to argue – as Dr. Harris does -- that the U.S. government did not want to go into Afghanistan is to engage in revisionist history. Dr. Harris fails to consider a variety of possibilities for going into Afghanistan that not only had to do with 9/11 but also had to do with, among other things, that country's potential for serving as a strategic location for building a gas pipe line.

101

For example, the events of 9/11 could have been a pretext for, among other things, invading Afghanistan, and, thereby, getting the war on terror started. The events of 9/11 could have been a pretext for: Passing of The Patriot Act, and/or for establishing Homeland Security, and/or for enabling various intelligence agencies to conduct ever more rigorous forms of illegal surveillance on the American people, and/or for justifying programs of rendition and torture. … all of which were in place prior to the invasion of Iraq.

The events of 9/11 might also have been a pretext for justifying the elimination of the Taliban's interference with the heroin drug trade. In addition, the events of 9/11 could have been a pretext for generating huge spending increases in the military budget and, therefore, increasing profits for the military-industrial complex.

The events of 9/11 might have been a pretext for undermining criticism of, and opposition to, the idea of further wars in the Middle East. Consequently, the events of 9/11 could have helped grease the skids for sliding into the invasion of Iraq.

Harris focuses on the fact that citing 9/11 as a pretext for invading Iraq makes no sense. However, he fails to consider all of the things that the events of 9/11 enabled the federal government to do quite independently of Iraq and for which 9/11 could have served as a pretext for initiating.

Dr. Harris continues on during the Joe Rogan interview with the following comment:

"We go to Iraq … that worked out well … the idea that that was the easiest way to get their oil is crazy. It would have been far cheaper to buy it.

Dr. Harris's foregoing analysis is quite off the mark. Saddam Hussein was interested in accepting, and had begun transitioning into, a program of receiving, Euros in payment for oil rather than U.S. dollars. This threatened the American petro-dollar.

If the petro dollar fell by the way side, then, this would have been the beginning of the end for the United States economy. Therefore, contrary to what Dr. Harris claims, purchasing Iraqi oil would not, ultimately, have been cheaper than seizing that resource if the United States were forced to purchase Euros with money that was not just printed into existence through quantitative easing in order to be able to pay for its oil.

In a relatively short period of time, the price of oil would have become prohibitively expensive for the U.S. government and American companies. This is because the monetary exchange markets could no longer be manipulated by the United States through pumping U.S. dollars into the world's economy in order to continue financing America's consumption of world goods … including oil.

The only thing crazy here is Harris's analysis of the Iraq situation. The reason for invading Iraq was not just about oil but, even more fundamentally, was about controlling the cost – and, therefore, affordability -- of oil in America.

During the Joe Rogan interview, Dr. Harris stated that:

"If we just wanted to go into Iraq to create … let's buy the idea that people conspire and that, actually, certain people in our government are willing to run a false flag operation so that we can go into Iraq. What would you have done? You would have shot down one of our planes over Iraq … we wouldn't even have needed that because Saddam was shooting at our planes … we had a no-fly zone in force for ten years … the war wasn't over as far as he was concerned … he kept shooting at planes … he didn't hit any, but let him hit one, and, then, we would go in, but …"

Actually, contrary to the foregoing contrafactual thinking of Dr. Harris, the American government actually <u>did</u> run a number of false flags against Iraq. Those false flags went by the name of "weapons of mass destruction" and "Yellow cake" uranium from Niger, and the intelligence asset

"Curve Ball", and alleged 'high-level intelligence meetings between Hussein and al-Qaeda in Czechoslovakia', and the notion of Iraq being a primary source for "state-sponsored terrorism".

Dr. Harris adds on to his previous comment by claiming, in response to the idea that 9/11 might have been an 'Inside Job', that:

"... killing 3,000 people in downtown Manhattan ... people who were well connected and send the world-economy into a tailspin, it just doesn't have the right shape of it."

To reiterate some points that were made earlier, Dr. Harris's foregoing statement conveniently ignores a variety of possibilities for why some morally challenged individuals might not have thought twice about the prospect of killing 3,000, or more, of their fellow citizens, many of whom played productive roles in the world economy. For example, Dr. Harris seems to ignore the fact that the evidence that had been gathered involving the Enron, World Com, and Global Crossing scandals, together with various other market scandals, and were being stored in Building 7 of the World Trade Center, were all destroyed on September 11, 200. This could have served as a powerful motive for someone's being indifferent to any loss of life that might be associated with the destruction of such evidence.

Alternatively, one might wish to consider the multi-billion dollar insurance frauds that came about as a result of the destruction of the World Trade Center as an enticing motivation –– at least from the perspective of some twisted individuals -- for the killing of 3,000, or so, of the "little" people. One might also mention the profits that were generated by the theft of hundreds of billions of dollars worth of gold from the vaults of the Bank of Nova Scotia that were housed in the basement of Building 4, or the money that would be made from re-building the World Trade Center, as well as the money that would be generated through the military-industrial complex due to the destruction of the World Trade Center and using that destruction as justification for going to war, or the money that would be made by re-establishing the heroin trade routes out of the poppy fields of Afghanistan, or the money that might be made by mercenaries for the parts they would play in, first, Afghanistan, and, then, later on, Iraq. All the foregoing possibilities might have been far more pertinent to generating motivations for perpetrating 9/11 than either Iraq or whatever temporary blips to the world economy that might have ensued from the deaths of 3,000 people, irrespective of what the role of such individuals might have been in the world economy.

For some people, September 11th, 2001 was a tragedy. For other individuals, 9/11 was the mother of all financial, economic, military, political and/or career opportunities.

Toward the end of his interview with Joe Rogan, a question is raised about why the United States seemed so eager to invade Iraq, Dr. Harris states:

"To some degree, I'm talking out of my depth here because I'm not really like a policy guy ...

Nor, apparently, -- at least based on the foregoing three Internet programs -- is Dr. Harris "really like" a: History guy, or a "fact" guy, or a 9/11 guy, or a financial/economic guy, or a political analysis guy, or an "insight" guy. Furthermore, despite having received a doctorate in cognitive neuroscience, Dr. Harris does not appear to be much of a science guy either since he seems to be unconcerned with discovering actual empirical evidence concerning 9/11 and appears to prefer, instead, to become immersed in contrafactual meta-thinking with respect to various conspiracy theories that might have arisen in the minds of some people in conjunction with 9/11 but tend to be far removed from the essential issues of 9/11.

Many scientists who have abdicated their scientific responsibilities in relation to 9/11 might be like the previously discussed case of Peter Michael Ketchum, the former employee of NIST, who, unfortunately, up to a certain point in time, never really exercised due diligence in the matter of 9/11 because he had trusted – mistakenly – that the so-called scientists who actually were involved in the investigation of the World Trade Center destruction or the damage at the Pentagon were honest brokers of the truth concerning 9/11 … which they were not. However, although Mr. Ketchum needed 14 years, or so, to reactivate his status as an honest, objective broker of the truth in the matter of 9/11, nonetheless, he finally did become a scientist once again in that respect and started looking at actual evidence in conjunction with 9/11, and, then, proceeded on to analyze and weigh the value and significance of that data.

However, although Dr. Harris provides a certain amount of evidence to suggest that, to some extent, he has thought a little – very, very little -- about the events of 9/11, nonetheless, he has not done so as a scientist because the scientific method is entirely absent from the way he tends to engage the topic of 9/11. In other words, his perspective concerning 9/11 is not only almost entirely devoid of empirical content, but, in addition, the quality of his thinking concerning the issue of 9/11 lacks rigor, insight, rationality, and diligence.

As such, Dr. Harris does not seem worthy to be considered as an honest and objective broker of truth with respect to matters pertaining to 9/11. In other words he appears to have failed to make the requisite efforts to acquire insight into the nature of 9/11 in a manner that is rooted in a rigorous process that is transparent, open, not intended to evade difficult problems, or mislead and distort (through commission or omission) with respect to relevant issues, as well as be critically and fairly responsive to actual evidence

108

Like so many other scientists in America, Dr. Harris appears to have abdicated his fiduciary responsibilities to the truth in matters pertaining to, among other things, 9/11. In the process of having exhibited signs of willful blindness (see page 14) concerning the issues of 9/11, he has become part of the realm of "Unscientific America" that Chris Mooney and Sheril Kirshenbaum never talk about in their book of the same name ... namely, the realm of so-called scientists who have abdicated their responsibilities to the truth in the matter of, among other things, 9/11.

Perhaps, the reason why Mooney and Kirshenbaum never explore the foregoing sorts of issues in their aforementioned book is because they, themselves, suffer from the same malady as Dr. Harris does. In other words, they all seem blind to the fact that each of them, in her or his own way, is helping to bring about an "unscientific America" because of their unwillingness to be honest, objective brokers of the truth when it comes to issues such as 9/11.

The topic of 9/11 should have a central role in both scientific and non-scientific facets of the curriculum in every American high school and university. The fact that this is not the case constitutes an important reason why America is becoming increasingly "unscientific" because – as the issue of 9/11 demonstrates in the case of individuals such as Sam Harris -- all too many individuals who consider themselves to be scientists – or teachers of science -- have abdicated responsibility when it comes to fulfilling the most fundamental role of a scientist – namely, to serve as an honest broker of truth in all matters of investigation ... including the issue of 9/11.

<u>Noam Chomsky and 9/11</u>

Sometimes, because of his research in linguistics and theories of mind, Noam Chomsky is referred to as a cognitive scientist. Moreover, he has an office in, and teaches (or taught) courses at, an institution – M.I.T. – that is home to many colleagues who often are referred to as scientists or engineers and who have been helping to train succeeding generations of scientists and engineers for many decades.

In October of 2001, four or five weeks after the events of 9/11, Professor Chomsky released a book of essays called *9-11* that ran a little over 100 pages in length. The book consisted of a half dozen, or so, essays that were drawn from interviews he had done following 9/11.

Approximately ten years later he updated the foregoing work by adding an essay about a variety of issues that arose in conjunction with the Navy Seal Six operation that allegedly terminated the life of 'Usama bin Laden in Pakistan on May 2, 2011. The title of the latter book was *9-11: Was There An Alternative?*

With respect to the latter publication, I won't go into the details of the eyewitness accounts in Pakistan – not covered by Western media outlets – indicating that the American government's version of events in relation to the foregoing operation are not corroborated by individuals from Pakistan who actually observed Operation Neptune Spear take place at Abbottabad, nor will I do anything more than state that many years earlier (in 2002 or 2003) bin Laden had been reported, by a variety of foreign media outlets, to have died of various physical ailments, and, consequently, whatever took place on May 2nd, 2011 was something other than it was portrayed to be.

What remains the same, however, both with respect to the 2001 edition of *9-11* and its updated, 2011 edition, is that in both cases, Professor Chomsky tends to fail to carefully examine, analyze, and critically reflect on a great deal of relevant information concerning the events of 9/11 and the life of 'Usama bin Laden. Professor Chomsky claims to be putting things in an appropriate historical context in his two books (more accurately, two editions of one book), but all he actually does is construct a narrative that gives expression to his political and philosophical ideology.

Both of the foregoing works – without citing any evidence whatsoever -- take as a starting point the "official" government story that 19 Arab hijackers, working in conjunction with 'Usama bin Laden, planned and executed the events of 9/11. He, then, proceeds to engage in a historical analysis that purports to put the activities of the alleged hijackers into what he considers to be a proper historical perspective.

Early on in the first edition of 9-11, he says:

"The horrifying atrocities of September 11 are something quite new in world affairs, not in their scale and character but in their target. For the United States, this is the first time since the War of 1812 that the national territory has been under attack, or even threatened."

In other words, the perpetrators of September came from outside of the United States and attacked the home mainland of America. No provision is made for the possibility that there might have been elements of that attack which were orchestrated from within the United States by some rogue elements within the intelligence community, the military, the corporate world, and/or the senior executive service (the SES went into effect during the administration of Jimmy Carter consisted of a group of organizational, management executives who occupied positions just beneath various Presidential appointees and were intended to serve as liaisons between such appointees and the rest of the civil service.)

Professor Chomsky goes on to claim:

"The likely perpetrators are a category of their own, but uncontroversially, they draw support from a reservoir of bitterness and anger over U.S. policies in the region," and, then, he goes on to talk about the "moneyed Muslims" (such as business leaders, bankers, and professionals of one kind or another):

"... with ties to the United States. They expressed dismay and anger about U.S. support for harsh authoritarian states and the barriers that Washington places against independent development and political democracy by its policies of 'propping up oppressive regimes."

The foregoing comments constitute part of the core set of forces that supposedly induced "the likely perpetrators" (i.e., Muslims) to commit the atrocities of September 11. Yet, the narrative that is being constructed by Professor Chomsky is done in the absence of any evidence indicating that Muslims actually carried out the acts of 9/11, and, moreover, the hermeneutical tapestry that is being woven by Professor Chomsky does not offer any evidence – other than presumed motives – that are capable of lending support to the idea that one should consider the 19 Arabs who were identified by the FBI (and who did so within a matter of hours) as the perpetrators of 9/11 or why one should consider them to be "the likely perpetrators".

Much of the book, *9-11*, consists in a litany of variations on the same foregoing themes – namely, how the imperialistic, as well as financially and economically exploitive policies of the United States in different parts of the world and in different periods of history have helped bring about a multiplicity of powders kegs of resentment, anger, and bitterness concerning the United States … especially in the Muslim world. However, at no point during the process of advancing any of the foregoing instances of analysis does Professor Chomsky cite one piece of evidence indicating that Muslims actually were responsible for the atrocities of 9/11.

He is like a detective who says again and again and again: 'Well, they certainly had the motive to do it. We gave it to them." Nonetheless, he does not produce any forensic evidence that has probative value.

Professor Chomsky goes on to say:

"…it is important not to be intimidated by hysterical ranting and lies and to keep as closely as one can to the course of truth and honesty and concern for the human consequences of what one does, or fails to do."

Yet, as I believe will become clear in due course, Professor Chomsky is the one who is guilty of hysterical ranting and, quite miserably, fails "to keep as closely as one can to the course of truth and honesty and concern for the human consequences of what one does, or fails to do" when it comes to the issue of 9/11.

Later in his book, Professor Chomsky states in response to the question of 'Who is responsible' for 9/11, he answers:

"... It was assumed, plausibly, that the guilty parties were bin Laden and his al-Qaeda network."

Unfortunately, Professor Chomsky never provides an account – either in this book or in others that he has written – capable of demonstrating -- in terms of hard evidence -- what makes such an assumption plausible, other than to say that "No one knows more about them (i.e., al-Qaeda) than the CIA" ... something that we have to take at face value because evidence is never forthcoming to indicate that the CIA either knew them as well as they claimed or knew them in a way that was capable of proving that bin Laden and his al-Qaeda network were responsible for 9/11.

In fact, during *"An Evening with Noam Chomsky: The War On Terror"* that took place at M.I.T. on October 18th, 2001, Professor Chomsky indicated that while he, more or less, agreed with the official position of the Bush Administration concerning the alleged identity of the perpetrators of 9/11, nonetheless, "...it was astonishing to see how weak the evidence was," and, then, went on to suggest that for purposes of discussion he was going to assume that such an account was true but, whether, or not, Islamic terrorists were involved in 9/11 didn't matter much.

What an astonishing thing to say. This is comparable to a system of justice sentencing someone to a life sentence in prison or sentencing them to death and, then, adding, that whether, or not, the person being sentenced in the foregoing manner is guilty doesn't matter much.

How does one justify such a statement? I have, yet, to come across anything in Professor Chomsky's books or presentations that is capable of justifying his claim that whether, or not, Islamic terrorists perpetrated the atrocities of 9/11 doesn't matter.

What is equally astonishing is the utter lack of curiosity that Professor Chomsky seems to exhibit in relation to the fact, by his own admission, that the evidence concerning the alleged guilt of al-Qaeda and bin Laden appeared to be so weak. Why did he just slide pass this issue of weak evidence and proceed to work on the assumption that not only were the allegations true, but, when push came to shove, whether, or not, Muslim terrorists were involved didn't matter?

One could assume that Professor Chomsky feels that the most important aspect of his analysis has to do with providing insight into, and an understanding (i.e. a proper historical perspective) of, the United States and the way in which its political, financial, military, and economic policies create problems that, sooner or later, will have unwanted consequences for both the United States and the world ... one of which was 9/11. From such a perspective, the sort of terrorism that is entailed by groups like al-Qaeda is, relatively speaking, small potatoes when measured against the terrorist activities perpetrated by the United States, and, in this respect, whether Muslim terrorists perpetrated 9/11 doesn't really matter ... what matters are U.S. policies and their problematic ramifications ... both domestically and internationally.

However, if Professor Chomsky is wrong in his analysis of the nature of the events that are taking place in the world and/or why those events are occurring – and I believe he is – then, identifying who actually perpetrated the atrocities of 9/11 really will matter. In fact, Professor Chomsky's flawed analysis of 9/11 serves as proof that either he really doesn't understand why identifying the actual perpetrators of 9/11 is of fundamental importance for gaining insight into the nature of world dynamics or, alternatively, he actually does understand the significance of this issue and chooses to hide the truth as well as be less than honest with respect to his analysis of the 9/11 tragedy and, as a result, he has failed to adhere to his set of previously noted values – namely, "...to keep as closely as one can to the course of truth and honesty and concern for the human consequences of what one does, or fails to do."

According to Professor Chomsky, individuals who believe that the "official" story concerning 9/11 is suspect or who believe they have uncovered evidence to demonstrate that the "official" story is, in some way, untenable should do what any scientist does – namely, publish their findings in the available scientific and professional journals and arrange talks at various universities to address those issues. Apparently, Professor Chomsky does not know as much about science as his place of employment might suggest because the world he inhabits – that Is, the realm of science, engineering and academia -- is not always a bastion for the free flow of information, essential curiosity, rigorous research, and/or objective analysis that he seems to believe it is.

A number of scientists – for example, Judy Wood, Steven Jones, Kevin Ryan, and Niels Harrit – lost their jobs because they questioned the "official" position concerning 9/11. Once people start losing their jobs for engaging in a process of critical inquiry concerning 9/11 – or, any number of topics – the influenza of self-censorship begins to spread fairly quickly among previously inquiring minds.

Furthermore, the fact there were many scientists and engineers associated with NIST, *Scientific American*, *The Pentagon Performance Report*, and *Popular Mechanics* didn't prevent those individuals from issuing articles, books, and reports that were breathtaking in their ineptitude and the extent to which those individuals betrayed the tenets of objective inquiry. Yet, the foregoing sort of mentality almost completely dominates the activities of many scientific, professional, media, and academic endeavors when it comes to, among other things, the issue of 9/11 ... and Noam Chomsky's way of engaging 9/11 reflects the same stultifying, incurious, group-thinking mentality.

During June of 2004, Professor Chomsky gave a talk in Budapest, Hungary. At a certain point during his presentation, the topic of 9/11 arose, and he responded as follows:

"Did they [i.e., the Bush Administration] plan on it in any way o know anything about it ... this is extremely unlikely. For one, they would have to have been insane, to try anything like that ... if they had, it is almost certain that it would have leaked out. It is a very porous system. Secrets are very hard to keep. So something would have leaked out ... very likely, and if it had, they would all have been before a firing squad and that would have been the end of the Republican Party forever."

In light of Professor Chomsky's activities over the last 40 years or so – which involves writing scores of books and articles, as well as giving countless interviews and lectures that provide, to a captivating degree, evidence-based details concerning the ways in which successive American

governments have consistently attempted to
subvert truth, justice, human rights, and
democratic processes, one is somewhat surprised
to observe Professor Chomsky become
preoccupied with speculating about the
'reasonableness' of Bush's innocence based on
something other than actual evidence concerning
9/11. Professor Chomsky has developed a
reputation for scratching beneath surface
phenomena in order to uncover the actual
dynamics at work in a given set of circumstances,
but, in Hungary, he abandons that modus operandi
and becomes ensconced in surface phenomena.

Consequently, Professor Chomsky does not
begin his comments, before a Hungarian audience
as any good scientist might, with something to the
effect of: "Well, let's take a look at some of the
actual evidence concerning 9/11 and whether, or
not, that data supports the government's
hypothesis because I have spent years
demonstrating that government's often cannot be
trusted to speak the truth concerning such events."
Rather, he proceeds by putting forth a straw dog
'who-done-it' scenario – i.e., Bush did it – which
enables him to avoid having to talk about actual
evidence and, instead, permits him to focus entirely
on speculating about whether, or not, the "Bush
did-it" hypothesis is reasonable given what we
supposedly "know" (??) about the phenomenon of
government leaks.

By framing the issue in the way he does, Professor Chomsky is able to sidestep the heart of the 9/11 controversy – namely, does the available evidence concerning the events of 9/11 actually support the government's official story about that day in which, allegedly, 19 Arab hijackers conspired with 'Usama bin Laden to fly planes into buildings in America. Instead, Professor Chomsky spends his time putting together an argument that -- quite effectively -- diverts attention away from key issues.

Furthermore, one should note that Professor Chomsky offers no evidence to substantiate his foregoing comments concerning the issue of leaks. For instance, he does not provide statistics about, or research concerning, the percentage of hidden government activities that actually are leaked when measured against those activities that are successfully kept from public view.

He merely states that the government system is very porous and that government secrets are very hard to keep. However, none of the foregoing claims are based on anything more than Professor Chomsky's assertion that such is the case, and, therefore, one is not in any position to determine how likely it is that someone would have leaked something, or other, concerning the government's participation in, or knowledge about, the events of 9/11.

Notwithstanding the foregoing considerations, Professor Chomsky also filters his previously quoted remarks through a conceptual framework in which one is not given any opportunity to consider alternative possibilities -- if the government actually were somehow involved in, or had knowledge about, 9/11 -- with respect to which part of government might have played an active role in helping to orchestrate the events of that day. Professor Chomsky restricts his focus to Bush and members of his administration, but if some other dimension of government were involved in the perpetration of 9/11 besides the Bush Administration, then, perhaps, one would be prudent to consider the activities of: Various facets of the "intelligence community" (something of an oxymoron), and/or different members of the military, and/or any number of possible candidates from among the Senior Executive Service branch of government ... none of whom – despite the fact that Constitutional theory suggests otherwise -- are necessarily under the control of elected officials such as Bush, Cheney, and company.

Professor Chomsky continues his commentary on 9/11 with the following remarks:

"... furthermore, it was completely unpredictable what was going to happen. You couldn't predict that the plane would actually hit the World Trade Center – it happened that it did, but it easily could have missed. So, you could hardly control it, but what you could be almost certain of is that any hint of a plan would have leaked and would have destroyed them ..."

The foregoing statement is factually incorrect in several ways. For example, at least from the early 1990s, technology has existed that is capable of remotely controlling commercial – and other – aircraft.

We are most familiar with such technology in relation to the phenomenon of drones. Nonetheless, prior to 9/11, both American Airlines and United Airlines (key companies in the events of September 11th, 2001) installed flight termination systems in all of their planes in order to guard against, among other things, hijacking and, thereby, enable people on the ground to be able to take over control of such aircraft if circumstances warranted it.

Consequently, if flight termination systems were activated on 9/11 by parties unknown (possibly unknown parties within government), then, one cannot necessarily say that "what was going to happen" on 9/11 was "completely unpredictable." Only people, like Professor Chomsky, who, apparently, are ignorant of such technological developments, might have been unable to imagine the possibility that what took place on 9/11 in New York, Virginia, and Shanksville, Pennsylvania might have been quite predictable – or was predictable to a considerable degree – as far as the individuals who were running those operations were concerned.

Professor Chomsky's foregoing remarks are also factually shaky when he says: "You couldn't predict that the plane would actually hit the World Trade Center – it happened that it did, but it actually could have missed." There are several ways in which such a statement is factually problematic.

First of all, Professor Chomsky is quite right that a pilot's chances of hitting either of the Twin Towers were very "iffy" propositions. However, Professor Chomsky apparently fails to appreciate the potential implications that his statement carries with respect to the issue of 9/11.

More specifically, at some point following 9/11, John Lear, part of the Lear jet family, described, for a Project Camelot film crew, how he took a number of professional pilots – including some who had many years of experience on the type of aircraft that allegedly crashed into the Twin Towers on 9/11 – into a Pan American Flight Simulator in Miami, Florida and discovered that under the conditions described by the FAA in its reports on 9/11, none of his pilots could duplicate what a bunch of novice Arab pilots, who had difficulty flying Cessna airplanes, supposedly pulled off on 9/11.

Lear referred to the challenge of intentionally flying a large commercial jet like American Airlines Flight 11 or United Airlines Flight 175 into a tall steel-framed building as being "impossible". He added: "At the height of my career, as proficient as I was in every kind of airplane, there's no way I could have done that. I mean, it's just too complex."

Dan D'vato, who flight tests pilots for his airline, also took a number of line pilots into a flight simulator in the weeks following 9.11. He tested them on a 737 -- which is a smaller and more maneuverable jet aircraft than the ones involved on 9/11 – and he discovered that despite many years of experience flying all manner of planes under all manner of conditions, none of those line pilots could hit the World Trade Center Towers at the speeds that were supposedly exhibited by Flight 11 and Flight 175 on 9/11.

Russ Wittenburg, a retired commercial and Air Force pilot, commented on the likelihood that the alleged Arab hijacking pilots of 9/11 infamy could have accomplished what the government's official story seeks to attribute to them. He said: "I flew the two actual aircraft which were involved in 9/11 -- The Flight number 175 and Flight 93. The 757 that allegedly went down at Shanksville and Flight 175 is the aircraft that is alleged to have hit the South Tower. I don't believe its possible for terrorists ... so-called terrorists – to train on a 172 (single-engine Cessna) then jump in the cockpit of a 757 – 767 glass cockpit and vertical navigate the aircraft, lateral navigate the aircraft ... and fly the airplane at speeds exceeding its designed limit speed, by well over a hundred knots, make high-speed, highbank turns, exceeding probably 5, 6 7 g's ... and the aircraft would literally fall out of the sky. I couldn't do it, and I am absolutely positive they couldn't do it."

Professor Chomsky never appears to question the idea that novice pilots who had difficulty exhibiting proficiency with respect to the flying of even single-engine Cessna airplanes (and, therefore, one wonders if one accurately can refer to such individuals as "pilots"), nonetheless, were somehow able to fly large commercial airplanes on 9/11 in a manner that experienced pilots would have had great difficulty in accomplishing ... if they could have done it at all. Why does Professor Chomsky consider the possibility that for members of the Bush Administration to try to perpetrate something like 9/11 would be "insane", and, yet, he doesn't consider the idea equally insane – if not more so -- that individuals who had been rated as terrible pilots by their flight instructors were subsequently capable of performing incredible feats of aviation on 9/11?

Furthermore, Professor Chomsky foregoing remarks are completely devoid of any hint of questions concerning the idea that planes actually hit either the Twin Towers or the Pentagon. The superstructure of commercial jets consists largely of aluminum, and aluminum is not capable of cutting through steel-framed and concrete buildings in the cookie-cutter fashion that is depicted in photographs of the Twin Towers on

9/11, and any reliable witness who has learned about what happens when an aircraft strikes a building will attest that this is the case.

In addition, aircraft do not melt into steel-framed buildings -- that is, show no evidence of meeting with an equal and opposite force of resistance, and, thereby, comply with Newton's third law of motion. Yet, this is precisely what is depicted in the 9/11 videos that, supposedly, show a commercial jet slamming into the South Tower of the World Trade Center.

Moreover, commercial aircraft do not disintegrate into nothing when they crash into an object – whether that object is a steel-framed tower, the Pentagon, or the ground in Shanksville, Pennsylvania. Yet, on September 11th, 2001, we are being asked to believe – and Professor Chomsky seems quite gullible in this respect – that four commercial aircraft disintegrated on 9/11 and left behind no signs of their presence ... except a couple of paper passports belonging to the alleged hijackers.

As pointed out previously, 80,000 pieces of the Columbia shuttle were recovered despite the fact that it was travelling at 17,000 miles per hour when it broke apart. Yet, airplanes that were travelling at 1/34th of that speed supposedly just evaporated into thin air since, for the first time in aviation history, parts to four commercial jets were never located following their alleged crashes on 9/11.

Some individuals have indicated that following 9/11 part of a jet engine actually was found on Murray Street near the World Trade Center. However, the part that lay at the foregoing location – and later on was moved to a landfill on Staten Island more than a year before the 9/11 Commission began its deliberations -- was a General Electric product, but United Airlines only uses Pratt and Witney.

Consequently, the jet engine part found on Murray Street could not have come from Flight 175 as some individuals have tried to claim. In addition, and, perhaps, somewhat more intriguingly, what was part of a General Electric jet engine doing on Murray Street, and how did it get there?

Professor Chomsky continues to expound on the issue of 9/11 before his Hungarian audience when he states:

"Now if you look at it there is a big industry in the United States … on the left as well… I mean you should see the e-mails I get … this huge Internet industry from the left trying to demonstrate … and there are books coming out … best sellers in France and so on that this was all faked and it was planned by the Bush Administration, and so on … if you look at the evidence, anybody who knows anything about the sciences would instantly discount that evidence."

While it might be true that there is a "big industry in the United States" taking place on the Internet in which various individuals put forth theories about how the Bush Administration perpetrated the events of 9/11 or how things were faked on 9/11, nonetheless, Professor Chomsky never offers any specific examples of what he has in mind when he makes the foregoing sorts of charges. Consequently, one is unable to determine whether, or not, he is correct when he says: "if you look at the evidence, anybody who knows anything about the sciences would instantly discount that evidence."

What evidence, exactly, is one supposed to be considering? Furthermore, just what aspects of science would "instantly discount that evidence"?

What about those individuals who do know something about science and did not "instantly discount" whatever evidence he is alluding to in very non-specific terms? Should one automatically assume that because some individuals might reach a conclusion that is different from the sort of conclusion that Professor Chomsky has in mind that, therefore, such people must not actually know anything about science?

Why should one suppose that Professor Chomsky's understanding of science is to be preferred to the understanding of science held by those who might disagree with him on this issue? Certainly, Professor Chomsky's comments do not offer any way to objectively decide such a question.

In fact, the foregoing assertions of Professor Chomsky are entirely vague in nature. This lack of specificity and concreteness continues when he adds to his previous remarks by saying: "There are plenty of coincidences and unexplained phenomena ... you know, why did this happen and why didn't that happen ... and so on,"

How can one possibly know if something is a coincidence or an unexplained phenomenon until one has an opportunity to critically reflect on actual evidence? Why should one accept as true something that Professor Chomsky says is the case just because he says it?

According to Professor Chomsky: "If you look at a controlled scientific experiment, the same thing is true ..." (i.e., as far as the presence of unexplained phenomena and coincidences is concerned). He goes on to say: "... when somebody carries out a controlled scientific experiment, at the best laboratories, at the end there are lots of things that are unexplained, and there are funny coincidences."

Is it necessarily true that at the end of controlled experiments carried out at even the best laboratories there are always "lots of things that are unexplained and there are funny coincidences"? If what he is saying is true, then, why not put forth even a little of the evidence to which he is alluding?

However, if an experiment is really well-controlled, then, there should be a relative dearth of "unexplained phenomena" and "funny coincidences" generated by such a process because that is what a well-controlled experiment is designed to eliminate. The data from an experiment should, as precisely as possible, either help confirm, or disconfirm, the hypothesis that led to that experiment being performed, and if an experiment leads to lots of "unexplained phenomena" or "funny coincidences, then, by definition, the experiment is not well-controlled.

Professor Chomsky goers on to maintain that:

"If you want to get a sense of it [i.e., that is, the issue of unexplained phenomena and funny coincidences], take a look at the letters columns in the technical scientific journals, like *Nature* or *Science*, or something ... the letters are commonly about unexplained properties of reports of technical experiments carried out under controlled conditions which will just leave a lot of things unexplained ... that's the way the world is."

While it is true that the letters columns in various scientific and technical journals do contain comments on various experiments that have been performed and, at some point, have been given written expression in the sorts of journals to which Professor Chomsky refers in the foregoing quote, nonetheless, such comments often tend to involve criticisms about aspects of an experiment that have not been well-controlled or that have failed -- for instance, in the analysis or conclusion sections of an article -- to take into consideration various **133** alternative possibilities that might account for the results that were derived from a given experiment. In other words, the comments in the letters to which Professor Chomsky is alluding in the previous quote often tend to be directed toward pointing out possible flaws with one, or another, facet of the methodology employed in a given experiment rather than being preoccupied with various "unexplained phenomena" or "funny coincidences".

If an experiment is written up and contains "unexplained phenomena" and/or "funny coincidences," then, such an article or note is quite likely to be flagged by the peer review process and required to be redone in a more rigorous fashion. Professor Chomsky's foregoing comments make it seem as if the idea of quality-control is absent from the publication of articles concerning scientific experiments, and in the process, he seems to confuse the dialogues concerning scientific method that tends to take place in various technical journals with the alleged existence of all manner of – but unspecified – "unexplained phenomena" and "funny coincidences" that supposedly appear in the letters columns of such journals.

During the aforementioned 2004 talk in Hungary, Professor Chomsky goes on to note that:

"Now, if you take a natural event ... you know, not something that is controlled ... most of it will be unexplained. There will be all sorts of things that happen that afterwards you can put them in some kind of pattern, but beforehand you can't ... and the pattern might be completely meaningless ... because you can put into some other pattern too if you want ... that's just the way complicated events are ... so the evidence that has been produced, in my opinion, is essentially worthless ..."

If the foregoing words of Professor Chomsky are to be believed, then, presumably, the 100, or more books, that Professor Chomsky has written should be considered -- that is, if he is to be logically consistent – as being "essentially worthless" in his opinion. After all, his books satisfy the conditions that he outlined in his previous comment in as much as those books explore an array of complicated, natural events involving history, politics, government, media, economics, language, cognitive processes, or philosophy, and, apparently, since, according to Professor Chomsky most of those natural events "will be unexplained", and, in addition, since "... afterwards you can put them in some kind of pattern, but beforehand you can't ... and the pattern might be completely meaningless ... because you can put into some other pattern too if you want ... that's just the way complicated events are ...", then, it follows that Professor Chomsky's 100, or more, books are little more than unexplained, meaningless, and arbitrary arrangements of data that could just as easily be explained by "some other pattern" of conceptual framing, and, consequently, should be considered to be "essentially worthless."

The choices before Professor Chomsky appear to be two. On the one hand, he could concede that the foregoing analysis of his position is entirely consistent with what he proclaimed to his Hungarian audience in conjunction with the issue of 9/11, and, therefore, anything that he says about such a topic should be considered to be "essentially meaningless," or, on the other hand, he could admit that his comments about complex, natural events constituting largely unexplained and meaningless patterns of thought that are fairly arbitrary in nature might have played a little too fast and loose with the semantics and syntax of the matter he was discussing.

Professor Chomsky brings to a close his comments on 9/11 in Hungary when he contends:

"I should say that I'm pretty isolated on this in the West ... a large part of the left completely disagrees on this and has all kinds of elaborate conspiracy theories about how it happened and why it happened, and so on ... but I think it is completely wrong, but I also think it is diverting people away from serious issues ... I mean even if it were true ... which is extremely unlikely, who cares ... doesn't have any significance"

Why should one accept his foregoing pronouncement that one, or another, alternative theory concerning 9/11 is "extremely unlikely"? He cites zero evidence that might justify his perspective concerning any particular theory, and he engages in no detailed critical analysis of concrete issues involving such evidence.

Instead, he spends all his time remarking on how the Internet and many commentators on the left are involved in little more than putting forth "elaborate conspiracy theories about how it happened and why it happened, and so on." This is nothing more than argument by assertion.

Moreover, one is somewhat nonplussed by Professor Chomsky's claim that even if any of the theories to which is alluding were true, nevertheless, according to Professor Chomsky, that fact would have no significance. One wonders what the nature of his argument possibly could be which held that if someone were able to demonstrate that 19 Arab hijackers did not perpetrate the events of 9/11, but, rather, those events were the handy-work of one, or another, facet of the United States government, then such a fact would have no significance.

Millions of people have been killed and maimed as a result of the manner in which successive American governments, the American media, and academia in the United States have interpreted the events of 9/11 in compliance with the official government story. Millions more individuals have been displaced as a result of those "official" interpretations.

Due to the "official story" concerning 9/11, the United States government has spent trillions of dollars on wars in Afghanistan, Iraq, and elsewhere. These are trillions of dollars that could have been, and should have been, spent on helping the people of the United States to improve economically, financially, and educationally, as well as to have access to better health care and an enhanced infrastructure, rather than contributing to the profits of the military-industrial complex.

As a result of the government's official position concerning 9/11: The Patriot Act was passed, Homeland Security was established; the TSA was introduced; a series of NDAA (National Defense Authorization Act) policy initiatives have been implemented; the NSA has stepped up its illegal surveillance of the American people; and a slew of Executive Orders have been written by several Presidents that, given the right opportunity, are designed to turn the American republic into a fascist dictatorship. In addition, the United States government engaged in rendition and torture programs in many parts of the world.

According to Professor Chomsky previously quoted comment, all of the foregoing events could have been perpetrated under false pretenses, but he claims that such a fact would have no significance. Just what are his criteria for defining

what constitutes the nature of "significance", and
what justifies his use of those sorts of criteria?

Professor Chomsky completes his analysis of
9/11 before a Hungarian audience by saying:

"... It's a little bit like the huge energy that's put
out on who killed John F. Kennedy ... who knows
and who cares --- plenty of people get killed all the
time ... why does it matter that one of them
happened to be John F. Kennedy ... If there was
some reason to believe that there was some high-
level conspiracy, it might be interesting, but the
evidence against that is overwhelming, and after
that if it happened to be a jealous husband or
someone else, what difference does it make. It's just
taking energy away from serious issues to ones
that don't matter, and I think the same is true
here."

What is the "overwhelming" evidence against
the idea that there was a high-level conspiracy
involved in the assassination of John F. Kennedy?
Professor Chomsky's foregoing claim – as well as
the perspective of the multi-volume Warren
Commission Report -- can be totally decimated
with 5 words – namely, "Back and to the left" –
because as is clearly indicated in the video of that
event, the fatal shot that killed Kennedy pushed his
head "back and to the left," and that shot could not

possibly have come from the book depository building where Oswald supposedly was positioned.

In addition, law enforcement ran Oswald through two gun-shot residue tests on the day of the assassination. Both tests were negative.

Jim Marrs (*Crossfire*), Peter Dale Scott (*Deep Politics and the Death of JFK*), Oliver Stone and Peter Kuznick (*The Untold History of the United States*), and James W. Douglas (*JFK and the Unspeakable: Why He Died and Why It Matters*), as well as Michael Parenti (*Dirty Truths*), John Judge (Coalition on Political Assassinations) and others, have all put forth considerable evidence indicating that Professor Chomsky's position is untenable when he tried to contend that the evidence that <u>stands in opposition</u> to the possibility that there was a high-level assassination plot against Kennedy is overwhelming. Moreover, contrary to the repeated claims of Professor Chomsky over the years (e.g., *Rethinking Camelot*) that the assassination of Kennedy had no appreciable effect on U.S. policy, the foregoing authors all indicate that the assassination of JFK fundamentally changed the direction of government policy with respect to an array of international, financial, economic, intelligence, and domestic issues.

The perspective of Professor Chomsky concerning the JFK assassination is fundamentally flawed. Furthermore, even if one were to grant his point that the Internet is filled with wild, unsubstantiated theories concerning the nature of

9/11, nonetheless, he also is wrong when he claims that even if true, such theories are of no significance.

To be sure, not every theory about 9/11 is true just as not every scientific theory is true. Nonetheless, in each case (that is, both in relation to science and in relation to the topic of 9/11), everything depends on the nature of the evidence that can be gathered, as well as on a proper analysis of that evidence.

However, since Professor Chomsky either tends to ignore actual evidence concerning 9/11 or fails to engage that evidence with due diligence, he really has nothing of value to say about 9/11. In other words, almost all – if not all -- of his statements concerning 9/11 are empty of substantive content and, therefore have no probative value.

In 1967, Professor Chomsky released an essay entitled: "*The Responsibility of Intellectuals*". It was published as a special supplement by the *New York Review* on February 23rd.

Among other things, the foregoing essay provides an array of details concerning the many ways in which the media, government officials, and technocrats tend to lie, distort, mislead, deceive, misinform, as well as commit sins of omission concerning the truth at the behest of power structures. Yet, rather ironically and quite inexplicably, despite more than three decades of driving home the foregoing point in a variety of books, articles, lectures, and interviews, nonetheless, in the aftermath of 9/11, Professor Chomsky never seems to consider the possibility that the media, government officials, and a host of technocrats were lying to, misleading, deceiving, or misinforming him and the rest of America in relation to the events of 9/11.

The aforementioned essay (i.e., *The Responsibility of Intellectuals*) also argued that the individuals to whom Professor Chomsky was alluding in his essay were in a privileged position, and, therefore, had a moral responsibility to critically, rigorously, and truthfully address the issues of the day. Furthermore, in that essay, he said: "If it is the responsibility of the intellectual to insist upon the truth, it is also his duty to see events in their historical perspective."

By failing to insist on establishing the truth concerning the issues of 9/11, and by being derelict in his duty with respect to seeing the events of 9/11 "in their historical perspective," Professor Chomsky has become actively complicit in helping to enable many of the political events that have transpired since the events of 9/11 occurred. As such, he has lost his right to be considered as an honest broker of truth ... at least in conjunction with the issue of 9/11, and, perhaps, in other ways as well.

Apparently, Professor Chomsky is an "intellectual" who – at least in conjunction with 9/11 -- has lost his way. If so, then he seems to have betrayed the moral and epistemological framework that he sought to bring to the attention of others nearly 50 years ago in his essay on the responsibility of intellectuals.

Some people might consider him to be a scientist of sorts. However, unfortunately, in the matter of 9/11 he does not appear to conduct himself as such.

Like the high priests during the time of Galileo, he refuses to look at the actual evidence. Instead, he seeks to dismiss, out of hand, such evidence as being of no significance ... even if true.

Nine years after his aforementioned comments concerning 9/11 had been delivered at Budapest, Hungary in 2004, Professor Chomsky again addressed the issue of 9/11 during a question and answer session at the University of Florida (November, 2013). He was asked a question by a member of the audience (Bob Tuskin) along the following lines ... namely, given that Professor Chomsky had said on Z-Net in 2006 that he (Professor Chomsky) wanted to see a consensus of opinion among architects and engineers with respect to the collapse of buildings at the World Trade Center on 9/11 and since over 2,000 architects and engineers now have agreed that Building 7 fell at free-fall speeds when it collapsed on 9/11 – and this is a point that NIST acknowledges – then, the questioner asked whether Professor Chomsky was ready to come on board with respect to the issue of 9/11 ... especially given that there is no better evidence of a media cover up than the events involving Building 7 on 9/11.

143

Professor Chomsky responded to the foregoing question by beginning in the following manner:

"Well, in fact, you're right, there is a consensus among the miniscule number of architects and engineers ... a tiny number ... a couple of them are perfectly serious."

Let's assume that Professor Chomsky is right when he claims that there is a consensus among only a "miniscule number of architects and engineers ... a tiny number..." Of the remaining number of architects and engineers, how many of them actually examined the evidence concerning 9/11 or how many of these other architects and engineers were, and are like, the previously discussed case of Peter Michael Ketchum, a former employee of NIST, in which he did not examine the evidence concerning 9/11 for nearly 14 years following those events because he assumed – wrongly – that the scientists at NIST who investigated the collapse of three buildings at the World Trade Center on 9/11 were competent in, and had integrity concerning, their investigatory efforts?

Suppose one has two groups of people. One group of individuals constitutes a majority of the architects and engineers in America who very likely -– as Peter Ketchum did for nearly 14 years -- might never have taken the time to examine actual evidence concerning 9/11, and another, tiny, miniscule group of architects and engineers who actually have looked at evidence concerning 9/11.

144

Why assume – as Professor Chomsky does -- that the consensus of the foregoing majority group of architects and engineers that might not know much, if anything, about the issue of 9/11 should be considered to be more important, or should carry more scientific weight, than the consensus of a group of architects and engineers consisting of a tiny, miniscule number of people who actually know a fair amount about the issues of 9/11? Professor Chomsky never appears to consider such a possibility but, automatically, assumes – without any evidence -- that the majority consensus view is the one that should be trusted?

Not content with merely saying that the consensus of architects and engineers who have adopted a contrarian position concerning 9/11 is a tiny miniscule group, Professor Chomsky introduces some ad hominem flavor to his comments by saying that "a couple of them are perfectly serious." I'm willing to wager that Professor Chomsky has not spent much, if any, time with any of the architects and engineers who reject, among other things, the conclusions that NIST reached as to the nature of the cause of collapse for three buildings at the World Trade Center on 9/11, and, therefore, Professor Chomsky is not in a position to know anything about the individuals whom he is maligning (i.e., all the architects and engineers who, according to Professor Chomsky, are not serious in their pronouncements concerning 9/11).

Professor Chomsky goes on to state that the foregoing group of architects and engineers:

"... are not doing what scientists and engineers do when they think they've discovered something. What you do, when you think you've discovered something ... what you do is write articles in scientific journals, give talks at the professional societies, to the civil engineering department at MIT or Florida or wherever you are and present your results, and, then, proceed, to try to convince the national academies, the professional societies, the physicists, and civil engineers, the departments in major universities, convince them that you have discovered something."

How does Professor Chomsky know – or does he know – whether, or not, the foregoing miniscule group of architects and engineers have tried to do exactly what he is indicating? Maybe the reason why their concerns have not appeared in scientific journals, or they have not been featured in gatherings of various professional societies, or their concerns have not been the topic of symposia and forums at places like M.I.T. is because out of fear, vested interests, ignorance, and various kinds of power politics that exist within the scientific and engineering communities, the concerns of the foregoing miniscule group of individuals have been ignored and effectively marginalized by those individuals who make the decision about what issues will, and will not, be explored.

Given that Noam Chomsky's name, along with that of Edward Hermann) tends to be associated with the issue of manufactured consent [derived from Walter Lippmann's 1921 (or so) book: *Public Opinion*, in which Lippmann refers to the manufacture of consent as a technique for controlling the views of citizens within a "democracy"], one can't help but be puzzled by Professor Chomsky's stance that the miniscule number of architects and engineers to whom he is referring haven't tried to do what he claims that they should have been doing in order to get people thinking about their concerns. Manufacturing consent does not occur just in the mass media, but takes place as well within science and engineering, and, consequently, one is inclined to believe that Professor Chomsky should have been among the first individuals to recognize that such power dynamics might be in play within the communities of scientists, engineers, and academics when it comes to 9/11.

Professor Chomsky goes on to say:

"Now, there happen to be a lot of people around who spent an hour on the Internet and think they know a lot of physics, but it doesn't work like that. There is a reason why there are graduate schools in these departments and research ..."

Once again, Professor indulges in ad hominem attacks through which he casts aspersions on a group of people about whom, for the most part, he knows nothing.

While it could be true that some people might believe they can acquire facility with the principles of physics by spending an hour's worth of research on the Internet, Professor Chomsky really has no idea what the academic and professional credentials are of the people who take exception with the "official" view of the government concerning 9/11, nor does he have any idea what research those individuals have done, nor does he know how much physics those individuals know and understand. Moreover, one doesn't necessarily need graduate training in physics – as Professor Chomsky seems to be implying in his foregoing remark -- in order to be able to understand various kinds of dynamics that are entailed by 9/11.

In many instances, one doesn't need much more than a high school course in physics and a little common sense to be able to follow arguments or pursue certain lines of investigation involving 9/11. More importantly, many dimensions of 9/11 don't necessarily require any formal knowledge of physics at all.

For example, the fact that the debris from the World Trade Center constituted a crime scene, and, therefore, should not have been removed without a proper chain of custody being established for it and without it being forensically investigated does not require one to have knowledge of physics. The statement that no steel-frame building has collapsed anywhere in the world due to fires either prior to 9/11 or following it -- does not require a knowledge of physics but of history.

The fact that Eric Lawyer, a New York City fire fighter, stated that NIST, along with the initial investigators, failed to properly protect the scene of the fires at the World Trade Center, and, therefore, violated national standards governing the investigation of the sorts of fires that encountered at the World Trade Center does not require knowledge of physics. In addition, the fact that initial investigators at the World Trade Center failed to comply with NPFA manual requirements in relation to evidence that suggested the presence of "exotic accelerants" (NPFA 19.2.4), alternative fuel sources (NPFA 18.15), and acts of extremism (NPFA 19.4.8.2.6) does not require a knowledge of physics.

The fact that William Rodriguez Kenny Johannemann, Jose Sanchez, Salvatore Giambanco,

Anthony Satalamacchia (all of whom worked at the Twin Towers), along with Felipe David (an employee of a company that serviced the candy machines in the Twin Towers) heard, saw, or felt the effects of massive explosions in the basement of the world trade center <u>before</u> the North Tower was hit by something does not require a knowledge of physics. The fact that 118 individuals (including many fire fighters and police officers) made recorded statements concerning the explosions they heard, saw, or experienced in conjunction with the events of 9/11 does not require knowledge of physics.

The fact that Barry Jennings was forced to walk back up the stairs in Building 7 on 9/11 because the floor below him had been rocked by massive explosions and that, subsequently, he and his companion had to walk through a ground floor area that had been devastated by explosions does not require a knowledge of physics. The fact April Gallop reports that she was at Ground Zero in the Pentagon when explosions took place, but when she led people out of the Pentagon, she saw no aircraft debris such as seats, passenger bodies, luggage, or fires from a plane crash does not require a knowledge of physics.

The fact that 17 people – including members of the Pentagon Police staff -- indicated that the plane they saw fly toward the Pentagon just prior to the onset of explosions at the Pentagon approached the Pentagon on the north side of the Citgo gas station -

- rather than the south side as reported in the *Pentagon Performance Report* -- does not require a knowledge of physics. The fact that no parts from any Boeing aircraft of the kind that supposedly struck the North and South Tower or the Pentagon have ever been found does not require a knowledge of physics.

The fact there are no Muslim names on any of the passenger manifest lists for the allegedly hijacked planes does not require knowledge of physics. The fact that training pilots have testified that Hani Hanjour – the alleged hijacker pilot of American Airlines Flight 77 -- approached them several weeks prior to 9/11 and demonstrated that he could not even fly a Cessna, and, yet, two weeks later he, supposedly, could fly a commercial jet in expert fashion, does not require a knowledge of physics.

The fact that 7-8 of the alleged 9/11 hijackers have been reported by BBC television to still be alive after the events of 9/11 does not require knowledge of physics. The fact that 'Usama bin Laden released a response following 9/11 stipulating that he was not responsible for those attacks does not require a knowledge of physics.

The fact that the FBI did not consider 'Usama bin Laden to be a suspect in 9/11 because there was no evidence tying him to those events -- and made several officials announcements to this effect -- does not require a knowledge of physics. The fact NATO requires evidence that a member country has been invaded in order for military options can be pursued but the United States never gave either NATO or the Taliban government proof of what happened on 9/11 does not require knowledge of physics.

The fact that, among others, John Schroeder – a New York City fire fighter – heard and felt explosions while working his way up the stairwell of the North Tower does not require a knowledge of physics. Schroeder reported that all of a sudden:

" ... our building got rocked ... we got bounced around in the stairwell like pinball's man, and we just said, you know what, it's time to go. We came down and it looked like a bomb went off in the lobby. Everything was exploded ... everything was gone, like what is going on here? For every window in the lobby to be exploded, I mean them windows were like as thick as forget it. They were 2-3 inch glass. You know ... come on. They exploded out of the lobby ... you know it wasn't from the jet fuel."

The fact that Mayor Giuliani's testimony also echoed the report by the Department of Labor concerning the existence of 2,000-degree heat at Ground Zero does not require knowledge of physics for one to be able to understand that something is amiss with the official story concerning 9/11. After all, if jet fuel burns at 800-1500 degrees Fahrenheit, and if, as NIST reported, jet fuel and office furnishings were the only source of fuel, but most of this had been eliminated within a fairly short period of time (as a result of the pulverization of almost everything that transpired during the collapse of three buildings at the World Trade Center on 9/11), then what was the energy source that caused 2,000 degree fires to burn for months?

This is not a matter of physics. This is an issue involving logic and common sense.

Professor Chomsky appears to label all of the foregoing issues, along with many others that have to do with 9/11, as being nothing more than factoids. Factoids are ideas or statements that are repeated and mentioned so frequently that they are assumed to be facts, and, therefore, to refer to evidence cited by those who reject the "official" government theory concerning 9/11 as being factoids is to engage all such matters through a pejorative, and very biased set of, filters.

No evidence is offered by Professor Chomsky to demonstrate that he deals only in facts whereas those who reject the "official" theory deal only in factoids. Like nearly everything else -- if not everything else -- that Professor Chomsky has to say about 9/11, there is an absence of evidence to support his position.

Consequently, Professor Chomsky's manner of negatively characterizing the abilities of people concerning 9/11 is little more than idle speculation. One can't but wonder why he feels it is necessary to stoop to such tactics of denigration.

153

Professor Chomsky adds to his foregoing statement by claiming:

> "... there is one article that has appeared in an on-line journal where someone claims to have found traces of nano-thermite in Building 7 ... I don't know what that means ... you [i.e., the person asking the question] don't know what that means ..."

While the foregoing statement of Professor Chomsky does indicate that he has knowledge, of some kind, involving an Internet article on nano-thermite, nonetheless, he, apparently, has not bothered to read that article because if he had, then he might have discovered what nano-thermite is instead of professing ignorance concerning the subject.

However, what mere awareness of the existence of an – apparently -- unread Internet article on nano-thermite does not entitle Professor Chomsky to do is to make assumptions about what the person at the University of Florida who is asking him a question knows -- or does not know -- about nano-thermite. He shouldn't presume that just because he – that is, Professor Chomsky – is too incurious to look up the meaning of a term --

say, nano-thermite – that, therefore, such people as the person who is asking him a question is also **154** equally incurious about such matters. Like many other things that Professor Chomsky says in relation to 9/11, he tends to be quite presumptuous with respect to what he believes he knows and understands.

Professor Chomsky continues on with his response to the question that was asked of him at the University of Florida about Building 7 and 9/11, He notes:

"Whatever one thinks about Building 7 – and, frankly, I have no opinion – I don't know as much science and engineering as the people who believe that they have an answer to this ... so, I'm willing to let the professional societies determine it if they get the information ..."

Professor Chomsky has no opinion about a 47-storey steel-framed building that was not hit by an aircraft but, nevertheless, for the first time in history, collapsed due purely to fires. Professor Chomsky has no opinion about a building that individuals such as Barry Jennings reported had been rocked by explosions prior to the collapse of the first tower. Professor Chomsky has no opinion about a building whose collapse NIST explained as a progressive collapse despite the fact that NIST also acknowledged that the building was in free-fall for more than three seconds and, therefore, exhibiting behavior that directly contradicts the notion of a progressive collapse in which each floor must crash down on the floor below in successive fashion and, as a result, provides no opportunity for freefall to occur. Professor Chomsky has no opinion about a building that fell symmetrically into its own footprint despite the fact that NIST's explanation for its collapse is asymmetrical in nature and should have led to an asymmetrical form of collapse but did not. Professor Chomsky has no opinion about the collapse of a building that NIST explains in a manner that is not capable of being reconciled with the video evidence of that building's collapse. Professor Chomsky has no opinion about how a variety of individuals (fire fighters, police officers, and news media) seemed to know prior to its collapse at 5:20 in the afternoon that Building 7 was coming down.

Apparently, Professor Chomsky, by his own admission, has no opinion about Building 7 unless that opinion is fed to him by "professional societies," and, therefore, he has basis for determining whether, or not, the story he is being fed concerning that building is true. How incurious Professor Chomsky seems to be in conjunction with Building 7.

Ironically, and rather tragically, Professor Chomsky seems to have become a cog in the mechanism of manufactured consent. He merely defers to the opinion of people whom he considers to be experts without bothering to determine whether that expert opinion is a reflection of sound evidence and impeccable reasoning, or whether it merely reflects the dictates of power.

By Professor Chomsky's own stated standards and principles, he has a responsibility to insist that truth be established. Yet, in any number of ways, he has reneged on that responsibility in the matter of 9/11.

Next, Professor Chomsky states:

"... so, whatever the facts [i.e., concerning the demise of Building 7], there is just overwhelming evidence that the Bush Administration wasn't involved."

One can't help be incredulous with respect to such a statement. In other words, if the facts of Building 7's collapse turned out to be due to, for example, the controlled demolition activities of agents appointed by members of the Bush Administration, then how could Professor Chomsky possibly try to argue that "... whatever the facts, there is overwhelming evidence that the Bush Administration wasn't involved" since those two statements would directly contradict one another?

Leaving aside the foregoing issue, what is the nature of the "overwhelming evidence" to which Professor Chomsky is alluding and that, supposedly, demonstrates that the Bush

Administration was not involved in 9/11? Actually, there is no evidence, per se, that Professor Chomsky cites in support of his contention that the Bush Administration had nothing to do with 9/11.

What he does do is advanced some speculative theories about why he believes trying to claim that the Bush Administration was involved in 9/11 makes no sense. In this regard, he cites three points that he considers to be uncontroversial and factual in nature.

First, he says that most people are agreed that the Bush Administration wanted to invade Iraq. Secondly, counter to those interests, the Bush Administration did not blame 9/11 on Iraq, the country that they wanted to invade, but, instead, they blamed 9/11 on their allies, the Saudis, and, the third uncontroversial fact according to Professor Chomsky is that:

"... unless they're total lunatics, they would have blamed it on Iraqis if they had been involved in any way ... that would have given them open season on invading Iraq ... total support ... international support ... a U.N. resolution ... no need to concoct wild stories about weapons of mass destruction and contacts between Saddam and al-Qaeda ... no reason to invade Afghanistan which, mostly, was a waste of time for them ... But, they didn't. Well, the conclusion is pretty straightforward -- either they were total lunatics, or they weren't involved, and they're not total lunatics, so whatever you think about Building 7 – there are other considerations to be concerned with."

Apparently, Professor Chomsky believes he sufficiently understands all the permutations and combinations of the dynamics that underlay strategic and tactical planning to be able to restrict his "facts" to the three he cites. Nonetheless, there are other possibilities.

To begin with, if Afghanistan were really a waste of time, then, the powers that be would not still be ensconced in that country after nearly 17 years. For instance, when the Taliban government took over in Afghanistan, it began to interfere with the lucrative drug trade that was being run by, among others, certain factions of the CIA, and, therefore, various political, economic, financial, and allegedly, humanitarian arguments were introduced in order to bring about war with Afghanistan for reasons that should appear to the public to be about something other than promoting the drug trade, and 9/11 was a perfect excuse in this respect.

Secondly, the Patriot Act already had been written prior to 9/11. Consequently, 9/11 provided great cover for implementing a draconian set of provisions upon the American people that would enable those in power to do pretty much whatever they felt like doing ... including war, rendition, torture, and Guantanamo.

Thirdly, contrary to the foregoing comment of Professor Chomsky, Afghanistan has never been a waste of time for the military-industrial complex. Afghanistan is one of many geese that are laying golden eggs for the profiteers of the military-industrial complex, and that complex tends to pull the strings of government administrations – irrespective of whether this is done in conjunction with Bush, Obama, or other presidential administrations.

Fourthly, 9/11 helped jump-start the whole "war on terror" meme, together with the many ramifications that ensue from that meme. Invading Iraq might have been on the agenda of the Bush Administration, but the war on terror was, and is, larger than Iraq and was used, and continues to be used, to justify an array of policies and activities beyond Iraq such as: Homeland Security; the TSA (Transportation Security Administration;, NDAA (National Defense Authorization Act) legislation, as well as wars in Libya, Syria, Yemen, and in whatever other countries the United States decides it wishes to exercise hegemony over.

Fifthly, although members of the Bush Administration identified an amalgam of Saudis, Egyptians, and Yeminis as being the perpetrators of 9/11 -- rather than Iraqi citizens -- those identified individuals were considered to be acting on behalf of al-Qaeda rather than the Saudi government. In this way one can both keep the oil coming and the war on terror going.

Soon, one began to hear about al-Qaeda in Iraq, and al-Qaeda in Syria, and al-Qaeda in Libya, and so on. One easily can charge people with being members of al-Qaeda, and as such, terrorists can be fashioned out of thin air wherever there is a need for them.

The Machiavellian machinations that were taking place within the Bush Administration went way beyond Iraq. The ramifications of 9/11 went way beyond Iraq.

Thus, for Professor Chomsky to try to argue that the Bush Administration wasn't involved in 9/11 because that event didn't provide it with a pretext for invading Iraq constitutes a rather excessively narrow characterization of some of the policy dynamics that were present in the Bush Administration and which could have served as alternative motivations for bringing about the events of 9/11. Many objectives besides invading Iraq were on the Bush Administration's list of things to accomplish.

Consequently, the "facts" that Professor Chomsky cites as constituting "overwhelming evidence" that the Bush Administration was not involved in 9/11 completely fail to exonerate the members of the Bush Administration. One could concede, without controversy, that the Bush Administration wanted to go into Iraq, and one can acknowledge as true the fact that the Bush Administration identified mostly Saudis as perpetrators of 9/11 rather than individuals from

160

Iraq, and one can admit that unless the Bush Administration consisted of lunatics – which it didn't – then, the Bush Administration should have implicated the Iraqis in 9/11 rather than Saudis. Nonetheless, despite conceding all of the foregoing facts as being uncontroversial, the conclusion that Professor Chomsky draws – namely, that the Bush Administration was not involved in the perpetration of 9/11 – does not necessarily follow from the stated premises because Professor Chomsky has failed to take into consideration an array of alternative motivations – some of which have been mentioned earlier -- for wanting to bring 9/11 about and, as such, could have served a plethora of ambitions that the Bush Administration had for America and the rest of the world.

Notwithstanding the foregoing considerations, one still might argue that although the Bush Administration, per se, was not involved in the perpetration of 9/11, it was, for unknown reasons, neck-deep in the attempt to cover up the nature of that crime. After all, among others, the Bush Administration failed to secure the World Trade Center and the Pentagon as crime scenes and, thereby, ensure that there would be a proper chain of custody in relation to the gathering of all evidence concerning 9/11.

Furthermore, the Bush Administration continuously resisted the idea of investigating 9/11, and it was the Bush Administration that, after succumbing to public pressure to form an official commission for the investigation of 9/11, made sure that the commission was underfunded as well as was provided with too little time, resources, and power to accomplish a truly thorough investigation. In addition, the Bush Administration was responsible for appointing NIST to study the destruction at the World Trade Center and was also responsible for not exercising due diligence with respect to the activities of NIST, and, similarly, the Bush Administration is responsible for the fraudulent activities associated with the *Building Performance Report* that was written in conjunction with events at the Pentagon on 9/11. It is the Bush Administration – via way of the FBI – that confiscated all public and private video recordings of the events at the Pentagon on 9/11 and chose not to disclose the contents of those videos to the public.

Moreover, to suggest that the Bush Administration might not have been directly responsible for the events of 9/11 does not mean that other facets of government – such as various members of the intelligence community, the military, the FAA, and/or the Senior Executive Service working in conjunction with any number of defense contractors – couldn't have played primary roles in the perpetration of 9/11. All of the foregoing dimensions of government benefitted from the opportunities that 9/11 set in motion, and, as a result, 9/11 served an array of purposes for a number of different facets of government that could have constituted motivations for wanting to

bring about – directly or indirectly – the events of
9/11.

When Canadian Barry Zwicker interviewed
Noam Chomsky on November 14th, 2002, the topic
of 9/11 came up and Professor Chomsky's reply
was: "Look, this is just conspiracy theory." Yet, in a
2002 book: *Understanding Power: The
Indispensable Chomsky*, edited by Peter R. Mitchell
and John Schoeffel, Chomsky is quoted as saying:

"... conspiracy theory has become the
intellectual equivalent of a four-letter word. It's
something people say when they don't want you to
think about what's really going on."

So, given the foregoing assertion, the fact that
Professor Chomsky told Barry Zwicker in 2002 that
9/11 is "just conspiracy theory", would seem to
suggest that, for some unknown reason, Professor
Chomsky doesn't want people to think about 9/11
because he, himself, uses the very term – namely,
"conspiracy theory" whose purpose he reported in
2002 was intended to induce people not to think
about "what's actually going on."

Like Sam Harris, the vast majority of
statements that Noam Chomsky makes about 9/11
are devoid of substantive content that is based on
actual evidence concerning the events of that day.
Instead, they both like to label anyone who rejects
the "official" story concerning 9/11 – i.e., that 19

Arab hijackers conspired with 'Usama bin Laden to hijack four aircraft and use those planes as weapons to in order to attack the United States on that day – as being "conspiracy theorists" or "conspiracy thinkers", and in doing so – each in his own way -- attempt to actively discourage other individuals from engaging the issues of 9/11 in a rigorous and critical fashion.

As a result, those two individuals cannot be considered to be honest brokers of truth when it comes to the issue of 9/11. In other words, the efforts of such people to acquire insight into the nature of some aspect of existence (e.g., 9/11) is not necessarily rooted in a rigorous process that is transparent, open, unintended to evade difficult problems, or mislead and distort (through commission or omission) with respect to relevant issues, as well as be critically and fairly responsive to evidence, and as such, both Dr. Harris and Professor Chomsky appear to exhibit signs of willful blindness (see page 14) with respect to the manner in which they engage the issues of 9/11.

Both individuals have made quite a few statements concerning 9/11 which indicate that despite the fact some people might refer to them as scientists, nonetheless, as has been discussed throughout nearly two-thirds of the present work, their respective pronouncements about 9/11 give expression to a totally unscientific way of dealing with that subject ... that is, when it comes to the issue of 9/11, they seem to lack objectivity, diligence, rigor, judiciousness, insight, discernment, or openness in such matters and, as a result, their judgment concerning those issues do not appear to be reliable.

I do not care to speculate about why they carry on as they do with respect to 9/11. I only know that I do not trust what they have to say in relation to either 9/11 or any matter that is affected by the ramifications of 9/11. Consequently, I do not consider them to be objective, honest brokers of truth concerning the matter of 9/11, and I believe there is an abundance of evidence to back up such considerations (some of which has been presented in the present work). .

Instead, I believe they are both guilty of exhibiting an array of active symptoms indicating that each suffers from what might be severe, and possibly, untreatable cases of willful blindness with respect to the events of 9/11. More specifically, given that neither Dr. Harris nor Professor Chomsky are stupid people – indeed, they are quite intelligent, although, clearly, Professor Chomsky is the more intellectually gifted of the two individuals – nonetheless, each in his own way, as well as in overlapping ways, could have known and should have known an array of fundamental facts concerning the events of 9/11 but, unfortunately, the two individuals appear to have chosen to evade, ignore, and discount those facts in a way that appears to have induced millions of other individuals (followers, if you will, of those two individuals) to have become equally alienated from serving as objective, honest brokers of the truth concerning 9/11 and, in the process, those millions of individuals also – like their leaders -- have succumbed to the ravages of willful blindness in matters pertaining to, among other things, 9/11.

Professor Chomsky, in particular, has left a trail of evidential crumbs indicating that his stance on 9/11 fundamentally betrays a variety of his own clearly stated values and principles. For example, in the 2nd paragraph of his 1967 essay, 'The Responsibility of Intellectuals,' Professor Chomsky states:

"Intellectuals are in a position to expose the lies of governments, to analyze actions according to their causes and motives and often hidden intentions. ... For a privileged minority, Western democracy provides the leisure, the facilities, and the training to seek the truth lying hidden behind the veil of distortion and misrepresentation, ideology, and class interest, through which the events of history are presented to us."

Certainly, Professor Chomsky was in a position to expose the lies of government concerning 9/11, but, for whatever reason, he chose not to do so. Furthermore, Professor Chomsky was among the privileged minority who had "the leisure, facilities, and training to seek the truth lying behind the veil of distortion and misrepresentation" that was used by the government, academia, and the media, to problematically frame and filter the events of 9/11, to propagandize and indoctrinate the American people, and, yet, Professor Chomsky turned his back on such privilege, facilities, and training and, instead, appears to have taken a variety of active steps (both in some his books and in some of his public lectures) to help facilitate the process of distortion and misrepresentation being perpetrated by the government and media with respect to the events of 9/11.

In the 3rd paragraph of 'The Responsibility of Intellectuals' he maintains:

"It is the responsibility of intellectuals to speak the truth and to expose lies"

He, then, proceeds to describe some historical events (e.g., Martin Heidegger's pro-Hitler comments and Arthur Schlesinger's claims that the American sponsored invasion of Cuba was "nothing of the sort") that exemplify how intellectuals betray their responsibility to the truth, but, nevertheless, Professor Chomsky seems entirely oblivious to the manner in which he, himself, has betrayed his responsibility to truth in the matter of 9/11.

Later in 'The Responsibility of Intellectuals" Professor Chomsky observes:

"A good case can be made for the conclusion that there is indeed something of a consensus among intellectuals who have already achieved power and influence, or who sense that they can achieve them by 'accepting society" as it is and promoting the values that are 'being honored' in this society."

Quite ironically, in the matter of 9/11, Professor Chomsky now appears to be part of a consensus among many intellectuals "who already have achieved power and influence" and who have accepted the way in which social institutions involving government, media, education, and corporations have framed the issue of 9/11 and, as a result, he appears to continue to perpetuate the values (i.e., lies, distortions, deceptions, manipulations, and disinformation) concerning 9/11 "that are 'being honored' in this society by such institutions ... the very sort of activities toward which he was so critical in 'The Responsibility of Intellectuals' essay.

In the final paragraph of the foregoing essay, Professor Chomsky brings his commentary to a close with the following remarks:

"Let me finally return to Dwight Macdonald and the responsibility of intellectuals. Macdonald quotes an interview with a death-camp paymaster who burst into tears when told that the Russians would hang him. "Why should they? What have I done?" he asked. Macdonald concludes: "Only those who are willing to resist authority themselves when it conflicts too intolerably with their personal moral code, only they have the right to condemn the death-camp paymaster." The question, "What have I done?" is one that we will ask ourselves, as we read each day of fresh atrocities in ... "

not just Vietnam, but, more currently, Afghanistan, Iraq, Syria, Yemen, Palestine, and the United States. What has Professor Chomsky done with respect to 9/11 except, apparently, to be unwilling to resist the siren call of authority concerning that issue despite the fact that such power structures conflict intolerably with his often stated personal moral code concerning the responsibility that intellectuals have to insist on seeking and establishing the truth in all matters ... including, presumably, 9/11, and, as a result, according to his own stated values, he would appear to have lost his right to condemn the government for what he believes it has, or hasn't done, with respect to the issue of 9/11.

In the film *Manufacturing Consent: Noam Chomsky and the Media* by Mark Achbar & Peter Wintonick there is an interchange between William Buckley and Professor Chomsky that runs along the following lines:

First, Buckley refers to Professor Chomsky's book *American Power and the New Mandarins* and says:

"You say the war {i.e., Vietnam] is simply an obscenity, a depraved act by weak and miserable men."

Chomsky: "Including all of us ... including myself. ... that's the next sentence."

There are a few more comments exchanged between the two men, and, then, Buckley continues on with:

"You count everybody in the company of the guilty."

Chomsky: "I think that's true in this case."

And, then Professor Chomsky clarifies his perspective by saying:

"I think the point I'm trying to make, and ought to be made, is that the real ... at least to me and I say this elsewhere in the book [*American Power and the New Mandarins*] that what seems to be, in a sense, a very terrifying aspect of our society, and other societies, is the equanimity and detachment with which sane, reasonable, sensible people can observe such events ... I think that's more terrifying than the occasional Hitler, or Lemay, or other that crop up ... these people would not be able to operate if not for this apathy and equanimity ... and, therefore, I think it's in some sense the sane and reasonable and tolerant people who share a very serious burden of guilt that they very easily throw on the shoulders of others who seem more extreme and more violent."

Professor Chomsky's concerns with respect to the Vietnam War would seem to be resurfacing in the case of 9/11. More specifically, when one reflects on various comments that Professor Chomsky has made about such events, his words often seem to be remarks of equanimity and detachment in which, apparently, among other things, it doesn't matter whether Muslims did, or did, not attack the United States on 9/11 just as, according to Professor Chomsky, the topic of who killed JFK doesn't matter.

Professor Chomsky says things in such a "sane, reasonable and tolerant" way and, then, seeks to "throw on the shoulders of others who seem more extreme and more violent" (such as successive political administrations in the United States) a burden of guilt, when, there is a very real and terrifying sense in which the kind of indifference to, detachment from, an apathy toward the truth of things that seem to be exhibited by Professor Chomsky in his comments concerning 9/11 indicate that, perhaps, some of that assigned guilt ought to be shared by those – who through their sanity, reasonableness, tolerance, sensibility, equanimity, and apathy (as appears to be the case with respect to Professor Chomsky) – have helped to perpetuate the obscenities that ensued from 9/11.

If Professor Chomsky feels comfortable with referring to the response of people concerning the obscenities of the Vietnam War as being that of "weak and miserable" individuals who have become entangled in their own web of equanimity, sanity, reasonableness, detachment, and apathy, then surely, those individuals – as seems to be the case with Professor Chomsky – who tend to engage the events of 9/11 with equanimity, detachment, reasonableness, and apathy would also deserve to be included among the referents to whom his phrase "weak and miserable" might appropriately be applied.

Furthermore, one is dismayed to discover the ways in which Professor Chomsky has been perpetrating his own form of manufacturing consent in conjunction with 9/11 since, for so many decades, he has been warning his reading and viewing audiences about the ways in which processes of manufactured consent are used by the power elite to deprive people of what Walter Lippmann referred to in *Public Opinion* as:"The means to detect lies" (that is, the capacity to think critically and independently). Yet, Professor Chomsky appears to be deeply entangled in a process of manufacturing consent that seeks to induce his audience to defer to the opinion of professional scientists concerning the matter if **173** 9/11 and insists that those people who feel they have discovered something important about 9/11 should go to the institutions of power – the media, academia, professional journals – and seek their assistance to help address the issue of 9/11.

According to Professor Chomsky, people need to acquire the ability to detect illegitimate modes of control concerning the nature and flow of information so that those processes can be challenged and resisted. Unfortunately, his stance on 9/11 constitutes a major obstacle in relation to those who hang on his every word and, as a result, are prevented – as well as prevent themselves – from being able to challenge and resist propaganda concerning 9/11 ... propaganda that interferes with being able to access the truth about what transpired on 9/11.

Professor Chomsky maintains that the power elite have hegemony – or control -- over social and cultural institutions and use that control to distract, manipulate, misinform, marginalize, and unduly influence ordinary people through the propagation of various kinds of Necessary Illusions or frameworks of propaganda concerning the alleged nature of the society in which we live. Necessary Illusions are the myths and narratives that are fed to the populace in order to induce them to believe that certain things are true when this is not the case, but the consumption of such illusions is necessary in order for the power elite to be able to maintain its control over the people.

Necessary Illusions are meant to manipulate or deceive, and, unfortunately, this is what Chomsky seems to have done, and apparently continues to do, in relation to his comments and perspective concerning 9/11. For example, he puts forth one necessary illusion – namely, that Muslim's are responsible for the atrocities of 9/11 – and, then, he puts forth another necessary illusion – namely, that we can overcome our current political problems by ignoring evidence concerning 9/11 – and, as a result, the possibility of substantial change seems to recede from the collective grasp of many people who follow Professor Chomsky because the element of truth has been removed from their presence in the case of 9/11.

Near the conclusion of *Manufacturing Consent*, Professor Chomsky says:

"The question, in brief, is whether democracy and freedom are values to be preserved or threats to be avoided. In this possibly terminal phase of human existence, democracy and freedom are more than values to be treasured; they may be essential to survival."

I think Professor Chomsky is focusing on the wrong issues ... we should be focusing on the principles of sovereignty (instead of on democracy) and we should be focusing on the duties of care that are entailed by those principles of sovereignty (rather than on freedom per se). Furthermore, one of those duties of care is to serve as honest, objective brokers of truth concerning different facets of existence (such as 9/11).

Apparently, Professor Chomsky – who has been a long-standing proponent of a ideological system that weaves together strands of democracy, socialism, libertarianism, anarchy, and syndicalism, (i.e., an idea centered around the transfer of property, means of production, as well as the means of distribution to labor unions) – fails to realize that there might be something more fundamental than democracy, socialism, libertarianism, anarchy, and syndicalism. As indicated in the previous paragraph, this something more is encompassed by the idea of sovereignty (For those who would like to explore the notion of sovereignty further, please refer to my works: (1) *The Unfinished Revolution: The Battle For America's Soul*; (2) *Final Jeopardy: Sovereignty and the Reality Problem, Volume V*, and (3) *Democracy Lost and Regained*).

Professor Chomsky believes that in order to overcome the Propaganda Model that the power elite use to convey various Necessary Illusions to the citizens in an attempt to induce the latter group of people to become compliant with the way of power, citizens must take two crucial actions. First, citizens should seek information from alternative media rather than from sources that are firmly ensconced in the operations of the propaganda mill that serves the interests of the power elite, and, secondly, citizens need to become involved in grassroots community action through which they work, in concert with one another, toward establishing some sort of libertarian-socialist-syndicalist-anarchist political and economic system through which to realize, at least in part, the inherent potential for creativity that Professor Chomsky believes people, in general, possess.

However, media literacy involves something more than just seeking out alternative media sources. Media literacy is about developing a capacity to be independent with respect to the process of critically reflecting on all media options … including the alternative media.

In short, one must do one's own research. In addition, one is responsible for exercising due diligence and, therefore, engaging in a process of critical reflection concerning such information irrespective of its source.

In my opinion, Professor Chomsky fails his followers in an essential way in conjunction with the foregoing issue. More specifically, Professor Chomsky is supposedly interested in helping people to become disengaged from systems of propaganda and, as a result, develop independence of thought. Yet, Professor Chomsky seems to have abdicated his responsibility to assist many, if any, of his followers, to develop the sort of intellectual independence that would enable those individuals to be able to identify and challenge Professor Chomsky's own system for generating propaganda and manufacturing consent concerning the events of 9/11.

By failing to exercise due diligence with respect to the events of 9/11, Professor Chomsky would seem to have denied his followers the very thing they might need – i.e., the truth -- to serve as a seed from which grassroots community action could grow, and, as a result, he sabotages his own proposal for how to overcome the Propaganda Model of the prevailing power elite. Instead, Professor Chomsky appears to have offered his followers little more than several Necessary Illusions (e.g., that 19 Arabs perpetrated the atrocities of 9/11 and that the truth doesn't matter when it comes to 9/11) that appear to be designed to establish and maintain his own ideological hegemony or control over the conversation concerning our collective futures.

As previously noted, Professor Chomsky claims toward the end of *Manufacturing Consent* that: "Democracy and freedom are more than values to be treasured; they may be essential to survival." Nonetheless, a value that is to be treasured even more than democracy and freedom, and, as well, a value that is even more essential to our survival than democracy and freedom is the truth ... the very value that Professor Chomsky seems to want to jettison when it comes to the issue of 9/11.

Without truth, neither democracy nor freedom is possible. Without truth, survival becomes corrupt.

Professor Chomsky could have known the foregoing reality and should have known it, but, apparently, chose to ignore its importance in conjunction with the issue of 9/11, and, as a result, his reasoning process seems to have been captured by forces of willful blindness concerning that topic. The tragedy of Professor Chomsky is that he appears to believe that by proceeding as he does – i.e., in active denial of the actual nature of 9/11 – he is furthering his political agenda through persuading people not to be distracted by various truths concerning 9/11, but, in actuality, such an ideological stance merely undermines, corrupts, and delegitimizes the political and economic project he has been actively trying to promote for more than fifty years.